Foundations of Modern History

Foundations of Modern History*
already published

* A. Goodwin, Emeritus Professor of Modern History, University of Manchester, was General Editor of this series until his retirement from the position in 1975.

Nineteenth-Century Nonconformity

Ian Sellers

Edward Arnold

420268772 PQ

00167464

Text set in 10/11 pt Monotype Baskerville, printed by letterpress,
and bound in Great Britain at The Pitman Press, Bath

Contents

Abbreviations

The following abbrevations are used in the footnotes:

BQ   Baptist Quarterly

CHJ   Cambridge Historical Journal

CHST   Congregational Historical Society Transactions

EHR   English Historical Review

J Ecc H   Journal of Ecclesiastical History

JPHS   Journal of the Presbyterian Historical Society of England

PWHS   Proceedings of the Wesley Historical Society

SCH   Studies in Church History

TRHS   Transactions of the Royal Historical Society

JURHS   Journal of the United Reformed Church Historical Society

General Preface

In the course of the nineteenth century the character of English Protestant Dissent changed profoundly from what it had been in the pre-Reform era. By the repeal of the Test and Corporation Acts in 1828 it achieved the right of participation in municipal and chartered company administration, from which it had been so long debarred by law, if not in fact. From being, in the age of the French Revolution, an alienated and hated minority, suspected of atheistic and treasonable Jacobinism, the Dissenters won their way to positions of respectability and power in provincial affairs which enabled them to influence the course of national politics without provoking resentment or unpopularity and to leave an indelible imprint on the social and moral ethos of Victorian middle-class society. After several religious schisms new types of popular sectarianism emerged to proliferate in different parts of the country, but, by the mid-century, not only Wesleyanism but Congregationalism and Unitarianism had all achieved greater institutional cohesion and confidence. Later, as the result of patient and prolonged agitation, the whole range of grievances—religious, educational, fiscal and social—from which generations of Dissenters had suffered, was swept away. More ambitious attempts, however, to achieve Disestablishment through various expedients, though successful in Ireland and later in Wales, foundered in England. During this period 'Dissent' became 'Nonconformity', 'Connexions' became 'Churches' and 'Unions' replaced schisms. In the eighteenth century Dissent had been a quasi politico-religious 'interest' on the fringes of national and regional politics, growing in commercial and industrial strength, but unable to win complete civic equality. In the nineteenth century Nonconformity was organized as a powerful auxiliary pressure group in support of the most successful reform movements and, from the 1860s it won unique political importance as the religious core of the emergent and later triumphant Liberal party. Though the 'Nonconformist conscience' was, in the last two decades of the century, a frustrating and divisive factor in political life, it was, nevertheless, a potent agent of philanthropic endeavour and social improvement.

Ian Sellers here presents a scholarly and sympathetic analysis of the chequered fortunes of nineteenth-century Nonconformity and gives his own fair-minded and informed assessment of the way in which the different denominations responded to the contemporary challenges posed by pauperism and privilege, the growth of Collectivism, scientific

Darwinianism and popular infidelity. His account of the evangelical revivals of the first half of the century and of the long-range consequences of the 'second Awakening' of 1859–1865 in the more professional 'revivalism' of the Moody and Sankey and Salvation Army missions provides a valuable clue to Nonconformist social attitudes as exemplified in the Temperance movement, its pacifist ideology and that distinguished charitable record of the Quakers, Wesleyans and Unitarians to which the author does full justice in his concluding chapter.

It may, perhaps, be said that the book has been conceived, not so much in the manner, as in the spirit of Elie Halvéy. The more detailed evidence provided by the author's own researches and those of other modern scholars adds, however, sociological depth and sophistication to the views here expressed, though these sometimes diverge from those of the great pioneer interpreter of nineteenth-century Nonconformity.

A. GOODWIN

Preface

In writing this short book I have been very conscious of the debt I owe to my former teachers at Ashbourne Grammar School, my tutor at Oxford, Professor J. S. Bromley, and to the two scholars, Professor Asa Briggs and Mr J. H. Y. Briggs, who supervised my research projects. More recently Professor W. R. Ward of the University of Durham has by frequent acts of kindness encouraged and developed my interest in the Nonconformist past. Nevertheless my greatest good fortune as a student of church history was to have been raised in the Primitive Methodist tradition just before that extraordinary religious ethos began to fade. I should also like to thank Professor Goodwin for his generous assistance, my colleague Mr P. Facer who kindly read the book in typescript, and my wife for her particular contribution to its completion.

IAN SELLERS

1 Itinerants, Denominations and Sects

Zion's travellers

Amid the vast social upheavals of the Napoleonic War period, itinerant preachers swarmed over the land. Awakened from their eighteenth-century slumbers by the trumpet call of the Methodist revival, Congregational and Baptist pioneers radiated outwards from their traditional Puritan strongholds, proclaiming a gospel of assurance to a populace overwhelmed with the pressures and anxieties of industrial and demographic change, plunging ever more deeply into hitherto un-evangelized fields, and more deeply too into lower strata of society than had frequented their meetings for a century or more.

Evangelism was usually the work of 'rounds' or local 'connexions' once again akin to the Methodist pattern. For the Congregationals, the Rodborough Connexion operated powerfully in the West Country; converts from Anglicanism, Methodism or Presbyterianism provided the core of renewed activity in Yorkshire; William Roby of Manchester revitalized Lancashire; 'Captain' Scott Cheshire and the West Midlands; a cousinhood of wealthy lay and clerical families London and the Home Counties. The Congregationals with good business sense and an eye to the future were particularly keen to establish village causes on the edge of towns with a view to providing a nucleus of worshippers in the event of future suburban expansion. In the towns themselves, moreover, tone could often be imparted to Congregational church life by the osmotic presence of a Countess of Huntingdon's chapel whose liturgical forms and genteel atmosphere and impression of being on the fringe both of the Establishment and of the most respectable Dissent won over persons of quality who might otherwise have held aloof.[1]

Socially the Baptists lacked all such advantages: their thirst for souls was if anything even more intense. They relied on a cruder, more un-compromising evangel and a more direct appeal to a lower social stratum in town and countryside alike. Strategic planning was foreign to them: the emergence of new causes through clash of personalities or theological disagreement was endemic.

For the Particular (that is, Calvinistic) Baptists, the lead in evangelism

---

[1] J. B. Figgis, *The Countess of Huntingdon and her Connexion* (1981). See also E. Welch's introduction to *Two Calvinistic Methodist Chapels* (London Record Society, 1975).

was taken by the ministers of Northamptonshire, especially John Ryland at College Lane, Northampton. The Western Association grew largely in response to Northants, while John Fawcett and William Steadman revived Lancashire and Yorkshire, and Charles Whitfield Durham and Northumberland. In London a remarkable trio of ministers, John Rippon, Abraham Booth and Joseph Ivimey, wrought a similar work. Meanwhile the New Connexion of General (or Arminian) Baptists, a youthful, vigorous body not yet forty years old, spread rapidly by means even more closely modelled on those of the Methodists, into the newer industrial towns of the Midlands and the North.

Statistically this progress was quite remarkable. By 1817 the General Baptist New Connexion was claiming 6,846 members in 70 churches while in the Baptist communion as a whole the numbers of churches grew from 652 in 1801 to 2,789 fifty years later. Congregationals who had between 1760 and 1810 increased in numbers by about 78 per cent had in the latter year 800 churches and by 1850, over 3,200. Even these figures do not allow for a number of causes, especially Baptist, which preferred to remain 'unattached'.[2]

The type of preaching which underlay this achievement was fervent exhortation rather than intellectual argument. The Congregationals, not notably a theologically conscious body, had no firmly fixed term for their doctrinal stance, but 'Fullerism' was the name given to the Evangelical Calvinism of the Particular Baptists after Andrew Fuller, their leading theologian, a tall, stout, muscular ex-wrestler, fearless and somewhat uncouth in his habits, an archetypal figure of the revival.

In Fuller's hands there was an attempt at system: he, like the Congregationals, Dr Bogue and Samuel Palmer, had, not without success, searched the dissenting past for a respectable ancestry for Evangelical Calvinism, avoiding those twin eighteenth-century pitfalls of religious rationalism and hyper-Calvinism (which is really rationalism in an exaggeratedly religious form), 'a perfect dunghill', as he had rudely described them. In the mouths of the preachers however such theological insights became empirical and pragmatic, pietistic and undogmatic, geared not to logical consistency but to evangelistic success. And this missionary vision, undergirded by an eschatology either post- or a-millenial[3] embraced both the home country and the

---

[2] R. Tudor Jones, *Congregationalism in England* (1962), 146f; E. A. Payne, *The Baptist Union* (1958), 19.

[3] Post-millenialism envisages the Second Advent occurring after a thousand year rule of the Saints, a-millenialism is suspicious of the idea of an earthly government of Saints altogether. Pre-millenialism, which does not figure extensively till the 1930s, expects the Second Advent to occur immediately before the rule of the Saints begins. It is important to note that the first two systems envisage a considerable time-scale during which the churches are called upon to evangelize the whole earth. The third system, yet to make headway in English Dissent, breeds an entirely different outlook, and demands the most highly personal and pietistic missionary strategy to hasten on the Last Days.

wider world. It was appropriate in fact that the Baptist Home Missionary Society (1797) should have grown out of evangelistic journeys made
on behalf of the Baptist Missionary Society (1792). Theological system
was brushed aside, cast into the shade by the irrefutable witness of a
multitude gathered in by rhetoric alone.

But it was not merely its theological content which perplexed old-
fashioned Dissenters about the new evangelism. Nor was it even the
untidy, bulging, utilitarian chapels of the revival (the first examples of a
truly vernacular religious architecture since medieval Englishmen had
clubbed together to build sanctuary or shrine) which contrasted so
brutally with the neat eighteenth-century meeting houses with their
charming 'quality of a well-scoured farmhouse kitchen'. Itinerancy was
destructive also of the age-old polity of Dissent. County Associations
were potentially at least a challenge to the sovereign independency of
the individual gathered church, which now became an instrument for
the furtherance of evangelism rather than a symbol of apostolic
purity.[4] The minister, too, became similarly instrumental, dethroned
from pastoral supremacy into the office of evangelist. Cottage meetings
and the ever present Sunday School likewise challenged the omni-
competence of the gathered church, creating religious republics within
a religious republic.

Finally the new evangelism tended to be a-political, again in sharp
contrast to the Old Dissent which had been roused to fervour over the
redress of grievances and the French Revolution, and had borne the
brunt of the anti-Jacobin reaction.[5] The one thing in common between
a hyper-Calvinist like the Baptist John Gill and a religious rationalist
like Priestley, two characteristically eighteenth-century figures, had
been their intense interest in apocalyptic and the immediate earthly
fulfilment of biblical prophecy, but writing just after the turn of the
century Walter Wilson, an old-fashioned Congregational with a sound
grasp of history, lamented the 'unaccountable notion' of new Dissenters
that 'the affairs of government should be left to the wicked'. (In fairness
to the itinerants their success had aroused enough government hostility
as it was without their gratuitously incurring suspicions of radical
intrigue.)

For older Dissenters for whom theological disputation was meat and
drink, the much-advertised 'funeral of bigotry' and 'triumph of
catholic Christianity' which the revival brought in its train proved too
much to stomach. Baptists in particular were seriously disturbed. Here,
on the socially-depressed right, hyper-Calvinism showed signs not
merely of lingering but of revival, and in the period 1800–1840 a new
denomination, the Strict and Particular Baptists, came painfully to birth.
Even amongst the children of the revival themselves disagreement was

---

[4] G. Nuttall, 'Assembly and Association in Dissent' in *SCH* vii (1971).
[5] W. R. Ward, 'The Baptists and the Transformation of the Church' in *BQ* xxv
(4) (1973)

always possible. Among Baptists a fierce debate raged over open communion after 1812, Robert Hall of Leicester, a keen advocate of catholic Christianity, recommending that the Lord's Table be open to all, members and non-members alike, as the necessary condition of all progress, even if eventually the practice led to 'open-membership' and the term Baptist was applied merely to individuals and not to churches; Joseph Kinghorn of Norwich taking a more conservative, denominational line in his advocacy of closed communion, that is the rite's restriction to church members alone.[6] But the Baptists, unlike the Congregationals, were a closely-knit fellowship. Their contentions, though bitter, were family squabbles which blew over in time. Usually no permanent breach resulted—even the most serious split, the division of the missionary society in 1817 which was occasioned by provincial fears of London machinations, had been healed by 1837.

Itinerancy and 'catholic' Christianity, its natural accompaniment, were eventually to wither in favour of a more closely-knit denominationalism, and the withering process was especially furthered by those very institutions which the revival had itself raised up in its train.

The triumph of connexionalism can be explained in a variety of ways. It may have been the local Associations, county-based in the case of the Congregationals (no less than twenty-one came into existence between 1781 and 1815), regional among the Baptists (and consequently fewer in number) which led inexorably to the creation of specifically denominational institutions. It may have been the considerable expansion of theological academies and schools or of denominational magazines where the overlapping and the need for rationalization pointed in a similar direction. It may even have been metropolitan impatience with ministers and laymen from the provinces coming up to the capital to beg for funds.[7] But possibly the most potent factor of all was the discovery that rigid independency was increasingly inimical to further evangelism, and led to vast and unfair disparities in congregational resources and ministerial emoluments.

Whatever the underlying factors, by 1813 the Baptists had formed a kind of Union, a fragile affair, without funds, badly supported and with the North grossly underrepresented, a social occasion for London ministers rather than an administrative dynamo, and advertising its purpose in 1832 very defensively as an organ of those churches holding to believer's baptism and 'the sentiments usually denominated evangelical'. (Perhaps this was, as D. M. Thompson suggests with his eye on the future,[8] a 'paradigm of the theological changes of the nineteenth century'. However, the Baptists embraced such a wide spectrum of theological opinion that anything more specific would probably have been divisive.)

[6] See A. C. Underwood, *A History of the English Baptists* (1947), 170f.
[7] G. W. Rusling, 'Dissenting Mendicant Friars' in *BQ* xxiv (3) (1971).
[8] D. M. Thompson, *Nonconformity In The Nineteenth Century* (1972), 7.

The Congregationals also, though their sense of separate identity was less strong (they had no such 'cementing factor' as believer's baptism, as an eighteenth-century Baptist minister quaintly put it) had, possibly because there were more canny business people in their ranks, thrown up large numbers of organizations for home, Irish and colonial missions, village preaching and church building purposes, and had thus come to realise by 1831 that a national union had become a necessity. It may have been, as A. G. Matthews once remarked,[9] 'blundered into', its declaration of faith was certainly, as Albert Peel described it, 'a diluted Calvinism, popular rather than scholastic, the work of preachers, not theologians',[10] and its inadequacies probably deserved some of the strictures which the great Dr Dale was later to pass upon it. The important point to notice however is that a body whose very name bespoke congregational autonomy had at last taken an embryonic bureaucracy into its system.

Quakers and Presbyterians were similarly affected by the all-pervading atmosphere of revival. The Friends of the eighteenth century in their sedate meeting-houses in the old commercial and market towns (their rural congregations had for the most part died out) clung to their habits of dress and speech as a barrier against the world, and to the 'inner light' as their peculiar tenet. Now, led by J. J. Gurney, a group of wealthy Friends, closely connected with the Anglican Evangelicals, endeavoured to make the body evangelically-minded once more, virtually replaced the 'light within' by the Bible as their seat of authority, disdained the 'peculiarities' in the interests of a wider gospel ministry, stimulated a renewed outburst of Quaker philanthropy and provoked by way of reaction a number of semi-rationalist secessions.

Amongst the Presbyterians whose wide-ranging theological proclivities had by now led them to adopt the title Liberal Dissenters a similar cleavage between the older and younger elements also began to appear. The older, well-established, unenterprising congregations, usually wealthy, intellectually dilettante and bearing their Arian heterodoxy lightly, saw growing up within their midst a more militant, dogmatic body of younger men, keen to spread Priestley's and Belsham's full-blown Unitarianism among the humbler classes of society—and by methods borrowed from the orthodox revivalists. Under leaders such as Robert Aspland and Richard Wright a new, predominantly working-class Unitarianism with its own missionary organization and popular journals came to the forefront, especially in the industrial towns of the north, despising the the Presbyterian name and looked at askance and even with downright hostility by the older-established churches.[11]

These latter were in their turn to move theologically though not

[9] A. G. Matthews, *The Savoy Declaration* (1959), 39.
[10] See A. Peel, *These Hundred Years* (1934), 69f.
[11] H. L. Short *et al.*, *The English Presbyterians* (1968), 236f; S. Mews, 'Reason and Emotion in Working-class Religion, 1794–1824', in *SCH* ix (1972).

socially in a very radical direction when Martineau and his friends, Charles Wickstead, J. H. Thom and J. J. Tayler, emerged to power in the denomination in the later 1830s. The bent of this 'Quaternion' was towards a Christianity suffused with Platonism, Emerson and romantic élan. They stood out as the intellectual elite of Dissent and spoke on terms of equality with Liberal Anglicans.[12] Secure in their sophistication they were distrusted and feared by all, especially the orthodox Dissenters for whom 'cleverness' in the ministry was tantamount to dangerous rationalism. Their learned quarterly, the *Prospective Review*, stood in lofty and cynical judgement on the philistine culture of the day, serving in the Dissenting world a role similar to that of the *Saturday Review* in society at large. The new, aggressive, missionary-minded Unitarianism shunned them with distrust as much social as theological, and from this period dates the uneasy joke that Liberal Dissent had two wings both of which it needed if it were to take flight.

But overshadowing all the other Dissenting bodies and inspiring them with evangelistic enthusiasm and organizational models alike towered the Wesleyan Methodist connexion. Unfortunately the missionary techniques and the psychological appeal which had borne Wesleyanism to a position of primacy within Nonconformity and to a point in the 1810s when it was seriously debated whether it would replace the Establishment as the church of the English people have not attracted the historians so much as its much discussed social effects, and particularly the personalities and tensions which it threw up once its success began to tail off after Peterloo.[13]

Thus, for the first half of the century Wesleyanism still remains synonymous with the person and policies of Jabez Bunting. To Bunting and his followers the body was totally different from the rest of Dissent, of which it refused to recognize itself as a part. It is easy to see why this should have been so. Under Bunting the connexion was fearsomely disciplined, from the exclusively clerical Legal Hundred and the Conference down through the Districts, the Circuits and the individual societies, to the classes and the bands. It was a holy community, whose very evangelistic success seemed to its leaders to depend on its Conference, the 'living Wesley', preserving the autocratic zeal of its founder, 'the oversight of a true primitive episcope', as Bunting called it.

To its enemies of course this was Romanism, and Bunting appeared as 'the Methodist Pope'. Willing and indeed anxious to employ lay talent in the financial administration of the body, and, at the lower end, in the spiritual leadership of classes and bands, Bunting at all times, but most notably in the Constitution of 1797, the Rules of 1835, and the financial restructuring of 1852–53, refused to countenance the

[12] D. G. Wigmore-Beddoes, *Yesterday's Radicals* (1971).
[13] An advance in understanding here depends on painstaking regional investigation such as that essayed by D. Gowland, in his Methodist Seccessions and Social Conflict in South Lancashire, 1830–57 (unpublished Manchester Ph D thesis, 1966).

principle of copastoral authority of ministers and laymen, and even the idea of 'lay delegation', that is representation, at Conference, District, or save in special circumstances, Circuit level. Resentment mounted.

Buntingism then is both spiritual ideal and disciplinary system. Yet as an historical phenomenon it has proved a source of continuing dissension among critics and sympathizers alike.[14] Firstly it has been questioned whether Bunting was a true interpreter of the mind of Wesley, as he claimed to be or deluded himself into thinking he was. Was not the Evangelical Arminianism which his friend Richard Watson brilliantly articulated against liberals like Adam Clarke a dogmatizing of Wesley's kindly, tolerant and enlightened theological outlook? Was not his high doctrine of the pastoral office and introduction of formal ordination in 1836 a right about-turn after a period of confusion, a harsh materializing of a tradition of catholic freechurchmanship, as E. R. Taylor described it,[15] or was it, as Bunting claimed, a formal expression of the most cherished of Wesley's spiritual insights?

Secondly, can Buntingism be properly understood without a glance at what was happening in the circuits? Was not this high clericalism forced on the bewildered ministers by lay grandees, vexed at the lowly 'societary' status of the movement within the Established Church? And did not the slow abandonment of itinerancy and the building of genteel chapels in the towns to the neglect of outlying areas provide much of the grass-roots support for Bunting's policy.[16] (It was the individuals and societies which experienced this feeling of neglect which provided the main rallying points of opposition to him.)

Thirdly, Methodism was affected like the other denominations by the growth of a centralized bureaucracy in London. This was often confused by earnest reformers with Buntingism proper, but was probably the inevitable result of a great undifferentiated revival movement settling down into some semblance of denominationalism.

Fourthly, there lies behind Buntingism the hidden demographic factor, the grim realization after 1816 that Wesleyanism could no longer aspire to be the religion of the urban masses, that its growth-rate was failing to keep pace with the rise in population and that it would be better to concentrate on quality, the edification of such converts as had been and could be made, rather than dissipate resources on winning ephemeral evangelistic success.[17]

Finally, though after the researches of Dr John Kent, historians should not make this mistake again, there seems to have been a continuing urge felt all through Bunting's life—and one committed to subsequent historians and commentators, notably Benjamin Gregory—to confuse Bunting's policies with his personality, to represent

[14] See J. H. S. Kent, *The Age of Disunity* (1966), 103f.
[15] E. R. Taylor, *Methodism and Politics, 1791–1851* (1935), 110, 122.
[16] W. R. Ward, 'The Legacy of John Wesley' in A. Whiteman (ed), *Statesmen, Scholars and Merchants* (1973).
[17] W. R. Ward, *Religion and Society in England, 1790–1850* (1972), 75f.

political issues as clashes of temperaments, or vice-versa. Bunting has been represented as an ill-tempered bully, a scheming Machiavelli, a dull grey bureaucrat: it is easy to forget that he was also a man of definite and widely-shared spiritual ideals.

The schisms which rent the Wesleyan body between 1790 and 1850 are a painful tale. The first of these tragedies, the New Connexion split of 1797–98, sets the pattern for the rest: a revolt which was essentially lay in inspiration and local in its demand for circuit or congregational independence and led by a distracted preacher, Alexander Kilham, drawing heavily on discontented local preachers and later on Sunday School teachers, slightly radical in politics, liberal in theological outlook, yet not averse to new-fangled revivalist techniques and affecting an air of superior rationalism and enlightenment, prone to sudden twists of fortune, internal controversies and catastrophic collapse, as with the quasi-Unitarian Barkerite schism of 1841–42.

The Leeds Protestant Methodists, the most aggressively 'congregationalist' and theologically wayward of the schisms, emerged in 1828; the Stephensite split, largely confined to Ashton-under-Lyne, in the early 30s; and the Warrenite or Wesleyan Methodist Association which began with loud democratic protests and ended with the usurpation of power by a layman, Robert Eckett, who proved even more of a tyrant than Bunting himself, in 1834–35. Here again there was the same sorry tale of desertions, as by Dr Rowland who had staged the protest originally over Bunting's plans for a connexional training college but who left after two years to become an Anglican, and of schisms, most notably the Question-By-Penalty case of 1850–51 which nearly destroyed the body altogether.

The last of the so-called Free or 'democratic' Methodist movements does however display some singular features, that of 1849 which was preceded by the famous Fly Sheets controversy and spearheaded by an extraordinary trio of malcontents, Everett, Griffith and Dunn. This revolt which led to a fearful bloodletting among the Wesleyans, the loss of over 100,000 members, only a few of whom joined the newly-founded denomination, the Wesleyan Reformers, was led almost in a spirit of resignation by older men, wearied with a system that commanded their loyalty no longer. It took five years to accomplish and was influenced by, though is not identical with, a bitter power-struggle in the Wesleyan hierarchy as a powerful faction endeavoured to displace the aged Bunting and his friends. By 1853 the last and most damaging of the revolts was over, and the Wesleyan leaders were left to salvage what they could.

Denominationalism triumphant

The religious census of 1851 gave Nonconformists ample cause for self-congratulation. The Quakers and Unitarians had made little progress, and the Congregationals despite their 3,244 chapels had grown less quickly than the other major denominations, having too many churches situated in the countryside and small towns. But the Wesleyans and other Methodists had advanced from an estimated 200,000 attenders in 1800 to nearly 2,000,000, and Old Dissent in general form *c.* 600,000 to 1,500,000.[18] Despite some disappointments in the agricultural shires of the south and in one or two smaller towns, Dissenters had clearly outstripped their Anglican rivals in most areas, particularly in those of significant population growth.

Strangely however there followed a ten-year hiatus before advance was resumed again, and the 1850s were fruitless years for most denominations, years of suspended hopes, marked according to the Congregational Paxton Hood by an absence of 'all present faith and belief'. It is difficult to point out the causes of this inertia. Maybe the grim Wesleyan experience of 1849–53 had rubbed off onto other denominations; high prices and emigration certainly took their toll, and dissenting ethics hardly coincided with the national mood of the Crimean War and Indian Mutiny. But the religious depression of the decade should not be exaggerated:[19] they were also, said Paxton Hood, years of 'experiment', when Wesleyans initiated outreach in the form of Home Missions, Congregationals in rural evangelism, and Baptists in special missions and services for workingmen.

By the time advance was resumed (whether as a result of the Second Awakening of 1859–65 or of the more mundane church building schemes launched in celebration of the bicentenary of the Great Ejection in 1862 is a moot point), Nonconformists were conscious that their ranks had been swollen by a number of new bodies unborn at the beginning of the century.

Two of these were Methodist, the Bible Christians with their stronghold in Devon, a revivalistic body with a marked holiness emphasis, emerging in areas not penetrated by the Wesleyans in the decade after 1810. James Thorne and William O'Brien were its heroic pioneers, Billy Bray its eccentric saint.

The Primitive Methodists' first leaders were Hugh Bourne and William Clowes, victims of Wesleyanism's hostility to revivalistic Camp Meetings, suspect alike for their charismatic excesses, their interminable length and their general social dangerousness. The Primitives arose in Staffordshire in 1812 and spread rapidly in gigantic pincer movements amongst agricultural workers, and in mining, fishing and other single-industry communities of Shropshire, Yorkshire, Durham and elsewhere. Its missionary preachers were cast in heroic mould, burning themselves out in evangelistic endeavour, dying young

[18] The best introduction to the census returns is still K. S. Inglis, 'Patterns of Worship in 1851' in *J Ecc H*, xi (1960).
[19] A rather gloomy view is presented by G. Best in his *Mid-Victorian Britain* (1971), 170–97.

or disappearing completely from the scene after a few years. They suffered because of their open-air preaching from mobs and magistrates, but attracted little hostility from employers whose labourers flocked to their support: they were appealing to a forgotten social class.

Bourne like Bunting was confronted by the necessity of organizing the infant denomination; the Tunstall Non-Mission Law was an attempt to edify the saved at the expense of reckless evangelism. But the preachers could not be restrained, and the Rule was broken or ignored. By the 1840s however the revival had begun to burn itself out: purpose-built chapels began to replace the hired halls and mission rooms of the past and the bucolic horseplay of the mobs was ceasing to plague the evangelists. By 1851 the Primitives were easily the second largest Methodist body, with nearly half a million attendances to the Free Methodists' 182,000, the New Connexion's 97,000 and the Bible Christians' 72,000.

The Orthodox Presbyterians too had by now established themselves on the English religious scene. For the most part they were Scots (though with significant numbers of Welsh and Irish), coteries of immigrants from across the border, 'who send regularly for their oatmeal to some remote region of the north that they may get it of pure grit', as one of their leaders put it. They, like the Methodists, were peculiarly prone to schisms over the question of church government. The great Scots Disruption of 1843 divided the Presbyterian Church in England from the much smaller Presbytery of England In Connection with the Church of Scotland. A third body, the United Presbyterian Church, founded in 1847 out of the union of the Relief and Secession Churches, was altogether warmer, more akin to Methodism, less nationalistic and more at home on English soil, voluntaryist and indifferent to the normal Presbyterian preoccupation with the establishment principle. Somewhat apart in its Caledonian exclusiveness, Presbyterianism was nevertheless more than any other influence responsible for English Protestant Dissent in the later 40s beginning to prefer the terms Nonconformists or Free Churchmen to the older term Dissenters.

Finally the 1830s saw the appearance of the Brethren, a scarcely noticed yet in the long run portentous development in Nonconformist history. Moderately Calvinistic, early Brethrenism was a movement of laymen and disillusioned clerics seeking in a particularly unsettling decade to be free from the ordained structures and ministry of the churches. The desire for a pure, apostolic 'one body' had led to the emergence of about 150 assemblies by 1851. The Brethren, particularly strong in the West Country where the influence of George Müller, A. N. Groves and Henry Craik was strong, were the Ironsides of their day. Their asceticism and bibliolatry were later to be painfully recalled by Edmund Gosse in his famous autobiography. They were rent with disputes over dispensationalism, the ordering of the assemblies and

Christology and in 1848 J. N. Darby's Exclusive Brethren broke away from the Open Assemblies. The larger body, like the Strict Baptist denomination which it resembled and from which it recruited, was held together by its leaders' personalities, by tracts and magazines and by common support of Homes, Orphanages and Missions. The Open Brethren, only one degree less markedly than the Exclusives, represent a stage in the gradual opting out of a large segment of the middle classes from the social process itself. And this tendency is even more conspicuous in that other extraordinary phenomenon of the 1830s, Edward Irving's Catholic Apostolic Church, and is certainly present, though less obtrusively, in the Churches of Christ or Disciples who spring up in the same decade.

Nonconformist development in the second half of the nineteenth century is almost wholly urban in character, and is closely associated with the evolution of highly centralized executive agencies within the the various bodies. Amongst Congregationals and Baptists this is particularly marked, as loose federations of independent churches were transformed into the provincial arms of burgeoning denominational bureaucracies. The Congrational Union, firmly settled by Algernon Wells, its secretary after 1837, was given a new and tighter constitution in 1847. It faltered somewhat, like much else, in the 1850s, but under the secretaryship of Alexander Hannay in the 70s and 80s and the new constitution of 1871, a policy of centralization of missionary and financial institutions and accreditation of ministers was actively pursued, and the way prepared for the adoption, almost without notice or protest, of a system of provincial moderators in 1919, whose authority if anything exceeded that of the Anglican episcopate. (Perhaps a warning of what was to follow had been given in 1907 when the Congregational Union ruled that small churches receiving financial assistance must employ only 'authorized' pastors. Yet no such restriction applied to wealthier, self-supporting churches.[20])

J. H. Hinton, secretary of the Baptist Union from 1841 to 1866, likewise transformed a rather uncertain and nebulous organization into a powerful and effective denominational agency. Augmentation and Annuity Funds were created in the 70s for the support of the ministry, and in 1873 a new constitution tipped the scales heavily in favour of the central organization as against the local churches. Accreditation, ministerial settlement and removal were brought under control in the 1880s, the Baptist Union Corporation Ltd. was founded in 1890, the Church Extension Fund in 1892 and the Sustentation Fund in 1898. Under the secretaryship of J. H. Shakespeare bureaucracy took a significant leap forward in the 90s, and separate, all-embracing departments of the Union multiplied. This elaborate machinery was

[20] S. H. Mayor, 'The Freechurch Understanding of the Ministry In The Twentieth Century' in *BQ* xxiii (7) (1970).

moved into more spacious accommodation in 1902 with the opening of Baptist Church House, whose very name would have been incomprehensible to Baptists of a former age.

Even more marked were the similar trends within Free and Primitive Methodism which had really begun as local and lay revolts against clericalism and centralization. In the Free Methodist body, which after the reunion of the Wesleyan Methodist Association with a section of the Wesleyan Reformers in 1857 took the name of the United Methodist Free Churches, the example of Eckett was not lost on his followers. The connexional Conference fell swiftly under the dominating personality of Richard Chew into the hands of a group of lay 'senators' and subservient ministers, while even the sacred principle of 'circuit independence' which acted somewhat as a counterweight to this trend likewise threw up its quota of controlling cliques of lay magnates.

In Primitive Methodism, which was vaster and more diffuse, a rather different pattern emerged. Admittedly the Primitives' Conference developed similarly to the Free Methodists', though it was more secretive, cabalistic almost, its inner debates unreported, its outward pronouncements formal and unexciting. But among the Primitives power was most highly concentrated in the Districts where lay leaders dominated over what Dr Currie has called their 'fiefs'. ('Districtism' was a word with special meaning for the Primitives[21]). Here bureaucratization, especially under C. C. Campbell, a Scots-born convert who imported Presbyterian discipline into the most charismatic and inchoate of English denominations, took a twist of its own, an endeavour through the promotion of ministerial fellowship, improved magazines and collegiate training, to raise the intellectual and social tone of the denomination. Stalwarts like Thomas Bateman of the Cheshire Round who recalled the pioneering days withdrew in disgust. Even the people's most precious possession, Hugh Bourne's Large Hymn Book, was not left 'unimproved'. After a number of disastrous experiments the authorities finally produced a definitive hymn book in 1889, dull, dry and formalized, a travesty of the earlier ethos of the movement. So completely in fact had the wealth of hymnody produced by the Camp Meeting revivals been ignored that a strong reaction set in, and the Supplement produced in 1912 was much more revivalist in tone.

Among Unitarians these tendencies were not experienced to the same degree. The movement was by now conspicuously divided into its two wings, and though the socially and intellectually exclusive churches of the Martineau tradition looked back wistfully to their 'Presbyterian' past, mistakenly finding in Richard Baxter a sort of Liberal Protestant born before this time, they made no attempt to revive the Presbyterian polity: their Conference of Unitarian, Liberal Christian, Free Christian, Presbyterian and Other Non-Subscribing or Kindred Congregations of

21 R. Currie, *Methodism Divided* (1968), 146.

1888 was perforce a very loose kind of federation. The missionary-minded, dogmatic Unitarians on the other hand, best represented in the later nineteenth century by Samuel Bache of Birmingham and Robert Spears of London, had had since 1825 their own British and Foreign Unitarian Association. This did not develop on anything like the scale of the Orthodox Dissenters' Unions: the newly founded Manchester College (1854) became more obviously a focal point for the working class congregations of the North and Midlands.

Late Victorian Dissenters were conscious not only of developing denominational hierarchies but were proud, too, of their social achievement. Even vis-à-vis one another a feeling of social pride was never far from the surface. The leading families of the Methodist New Connexion, the Ridgeways, Firths, Fowlers and others, felt a slight gulf between themselves and the Wesleyan Reformers who were in turn a trifle superior to the Free Methodists. Wesleyan shopkeepers were similarly contrasted with Congregational manufacturers. Yet if Congregationals felt themselves to be 'the cream of the middle classes' (and the names of Salt, Leverhulme, Spicer, Unwin, Remington, Mills, Colman, Samuel Morley, Crossley and Wills, all prominent in later Victorian Congregationalism, give some substance to their claim), the Unitarian elites were without doubt the 'Brahmins of Nonconformity'. Even the Orthodox Presbyterians, a small body but one which had grown very rapidly, drank in some of this new found elitism, loudly proclaiming in the 70s and 80s, as had their forebears in the 1640s, that at last Scotland was about to enjoy the opportunity of educating the English in matters theological and ecclesiastical, perhaps even in the ethics and conduct most befitting a nation of Protestants. But these were all divisions within churches whose social character seemed to outsiders increasingly uniform. By 1900, as D. M. Thompson remarks, Nonconformity was 'more homogeneously middle-class than ever before'.[22]

This pride of class and achievement could take the form of statistical boasting: the figures published by the *Nonconformist* in 1872, the unofficial censuses of 1881–82, the Mudie Smith Survey of London churches of 1904, all showed an impressive record of attendances (far less impressive, damaging even, if compared with total population growth). Yet it was the architecture of new church buildings which most eloquently demonstrated that Nonconformity had at last 'arrived'.

Even in the early part of the century urban Dissenters had imitated the Establishment by building warehouse-like chapels with Grecian fronts, or wholly Grecian chapels like Carr's Lane, Birmingham, or Great George Street, Liverpool. But soon the Unitarians, pioneers in taste as in ideas, introduced the Gothic style at Upper Brook Street, Manchester (1839), Hyde, and Mill Hill, Leeds (1848) and Hope Street, Liverpool (1849). Congregationals and Methodists quickly

[22] D. M. Thompson, *op. cit*, 15.

followed suit, F. J. Jobson defending Methodist Gothic against
suspicions of Popery in his *Chapel and School Architecture* (1850), and
J. A. Clapham Congregational Gothic in the *Congregationalist* for
1878.[23] Christ Church, Westminster Bridge Road (1872) was the first
metropolitan example of Congregational Gothic, Trinity and St John's,
Liverpool (1859, 1862) are among the first Wesleyan town chapels built
in this style. By the 70s, both bodies were also experimenting with other
styles, Romanesque, Perpendicular, Norman towers, doors and
windows. Internally too, stark simplicity yielded to fussiness: naves,
chancels, choir stalls, elaborate carving, side pulpits and reading desks
(sometimes with gowns and liturgies to match). This 'Nonconformity
of soaring spires', in Dr Binfield's telling phrase[24] proclaimed to the
world that the era of Anglican monopoly had effectively come to an end.

Yet not all the denominations could follow the highly respectable
Congregationals and Wesleyans along the paths of affluence and social
acceptability. Two in particular found it difficult to shake off their
heritage and were constantly troubled by memories of times past. The
Primitive Methodists were increasingly patronized by wealthier bodies
as the working class arm of Dissent. Interestingly, at the very time
when Joseph Arch was forming his Agricultural Labourers' Union in
the 70s, and the final blow seemed about to be struck against Anglican
landed privilege, such favourable references grew in volume. By their
fellow Methodists the Primitives were of course greatly acclaimed—
though generally held at arm's length when organic unity was men-
tioned: neither the Free Methodists nor the New Connexion wished
to be swamped by such a large and socially inferior body.

The Primitives did not quite know how to respond to this flattery.
They alternately boasted about 'being from the beginning a people's
church', and yet noted the 'growing intelligence, wealth and respectability' of their body, a process which was hurried on by the
Primitives' determination in the 60s and 70s to become an urban
church, and strike roots in the centre and suburbs of London and
elsewhere. The young middle-class leaders which this process threw up
played, however, hardly any part at all in connexional affairs.

The Baptists too felt a little awkward in the Dissenting world of the
later nineteenth century; both a tough, uncompromising 'character and
disposition' and an appeal to a more lowly stratum of the population
struck Charles Booth as a characteristic of the London Baptists. But the
'Baptistness' of the Baptists is a quality notoriously difficult to define.
They possessed a fair number of wealthy families and seemed to imitate
the life-style of affluent Congregationals and Wesleyans. (Dr Brock of
Bloomsbury, who persuaded London Baptists to come out of their back
streets and be metropolitan, was said by Dr Clifford to have been 'all

[23] H. Davies, *Worship and Theology In England. From Newman To Martineau*, 1850–1900 (1962), 47f.
[24] C. Binfield, 'Chapels In Crisis' in *CHST*, xx (8) (1968).

astir with the life pulses of the age' and to have regarded 'the Bible and *The Times* as the best material for the preacher'). Yet they could never completely shake free from the Calvinistic confessionalism of their Strict and Particular brethren whose very existence (the Congregationals had nothing comparable) was a tantalizing reminder of their roots. Consequently sweeping generalizations about them can only mislead: it is in the minutiae of denominational life that their quintessential character is most clearly revealed. Such is, for example, their attitude to white settlement in the colonies. For *their* colonial emigrants the Congregationals made elaborate provision at an early date: for the Baptists a Colonial Missionary Society was a non-starter. Pietistic, conservative and separatist, they refused to be enraptured by the expansive mood of the age. 'There's no place like home', declared one of their magazines à propos an elaborate emigration scheme being mooted in 1834.[25] A revealing episode also occurred in 1862 during the Tercentenary celebrations. A typically forthright Baptist essay on the event was entitled 'These Horrible Sectarians—Who Are They?' and ended with the heart-felt cry 'Long Live Sectarianism'. It is this stubborn, unyielding climate of opinion which helps to set the Downgrade controversy of 1888 in true perspective.

The Wesleyans, too, still remained conscious of their unique status within the Dissenting world. Yet all the pressures of the age drove this highly structured revivalist movement toward the liberalized denomination-type of ecclesiastical organization which Professor Martin sees as characteristic of later nineteenth-century Protestantism in all its branches.[26] It would be facile to describe this process as a movement from sect to church, for sectarian the Wesleyans had never been. Rather it is the basic unit in the connexion, the class, the central means of grace and the guarantee of its holiness character, which undergoes radical change, affecting in turn the entire denominational superstructure.

The freshness of the class system was growing stale by the 1850s. Various complaints were heard: the meetings were repetitious and boringly routinized, the leaders were inadequate, different social groups did not mix and tended to form their own separate classes. There was among some a desire for something less personal and introspective, more familiar and charismatic: others, noting the growing appetite for amusements in society at large, pleaded for something more 'social'. A bright, breezy fellowship meeting (such as that described by M. G. Pearse in his little classic *Daniel Quorm*) might reconcile both viewpoints. Young people in particular were shunning the classes, preferring a vaguer or looser church life, often centred on the choir, the Sunday School or even the recreational 'club'. About 1900 the most flourishing

[25] J. D. Bollen, 'English–Australian Baptist Relations' in *BQ* xxv (7) (1974).
[26] D. Martin, *A Sociology of English Religion* (1967), 77f.

classes of all were huge affairs of a hundred or more such as that run by Samuel Collier of Manchester, which of course were really mid-week meetings rather than classes in the traditional sense.

Despite eloquent defences of the system by Benjamin Gregory and others, the Wesleyans by the early 70s were seriously debating a credal or communicant alternative to the class ticket as a basis for membership. A long and at times bitter discussion ended in 1889 in an extraordinary compromise: the traditional class system be retained, but membership could be nominal. In 1891 the Connexion at last proclaimed itself a Church with a special underlining of its claims to a spiritual apostolic succession (a characteristic Wesleyan touch). In 1893 the words 'Wesleyan Methodist Society' were replaced by 'Wesleyan Methodist Church' on class tickets, and in 1894 a special service of reception of new members was introduced. A broadly-based nexus of semi-religious, semi-social Wesley Guilds, specially designed for young people, followed.[27] Bold declarations and a strident authoritarianism seemed to the leadership necessary to compensate for the growing laxity and folksiness within the congregations. Wesleyanism was now in church order and denominational outlook much more akin to the rest of Nonconformity. The gradual laicizing of denominational meetings and committees pointed in the same direction. A younger, more liberal faction, part clerical, part lay, grew up in the 1860s and voiced their demands through the *Methodist Recorder* (founded in 1861): by 1870 the theological colleges, the Book Room, Chapel Committee and Foreign Missions were under its control, and a demand for lay representation in Conference was heard for the first time. The high church conservatives, led by J. H. Rigg, fought hard, but to no avail. In 1883 the old *Watchman* newspaper which had belaboured the radical schismatics in earlier years was wound up: in 1877 lay representation had been finally conceded. A new radical journal, *The Methodist Times*, was founded by Hugh Price Hughes in 1885, and in 1893 G. E. Findlay's 'Church of Christ' effectively undermined the traditionally high Wesleyan view of the ministry, as voiced in the 60s and 70s by their most eminent theologian, W. B. Pope, thus pushing the body closer to the democratic Methodist sects. Only at the local level of leaders' and quarterly meetings did Wesleyan machinery remain in 1900 still uncompromisingly undemocratic.[28]

Despite these changes, however, Wesleyanism retained its pristine evangelistic fervour and its ability to confront changing missionary opportunities in a manner which ensured continued numerical growth. The earlier nineteenth-century Wesleyan initiative on behalf of sailors, the distressed, the rootless and the unemployed, a tale of

---

[27] B. E. Jones, 'Society and Church in Wesleyan Methodism, 1878–93' in *PWHS* xxxvi Pt. 5 (1968); H. Rack, 'The Decline of the Class Meeting and the Problem of Church Membership' in *PWHS* xxxix Pt. 1. (1973).

[28] R. Currie, *op cit.*, 164.

charitable and evangelistic endeavour lost sight of in the oft-told and wearisome story of the Buntingite political embroglio, was continued after 1855 in the Home Missions movement. The Missions have been criticized by Inglis and others as cheeseparing and excessively village-orientated,[29] but in the towns the Wesleyans' 'Mahogany age' (the 1860s) saw a thorough rationalization of resources after the recent troubles, and an effective penetration into suburbs of varying social character. In the 1880s and 90s also, the Central Halls with their back street missions were not only, as Inglis describes them, 'part of a massive and self-effacing social service operation', but a late outworking, perhaps the very last, of Wesleyanism's concern for the souls of the very poor. Dr Currie's picture of the Central Halls as the resorts of wealthy suburbanites, selfishly seeking oratory and entertainment, is wide of the mark.[30] If they are to be criticized at all, it is because their very success in producing habits of thrift, cleanliness and religious observance among the dispossessed led to such rapid embourgeoisement that their evangelistic thrust was blunted almost as soon as it had penetrated the darkest haunts of the great cities.

The challenge of the slums was one of the factors which underlay the movement for Free Church unity which became a Nonconformist preoccupation as the century advanced. The Presbyterians led the way: in 1876 the United Presbyterians and the Presbyterian Church in England, different in temper but undivided in matters of faith and order, came together in a sudden rush of enthusiasm after two decades of desultory talk. Though the smaller church surrendered the most, the union worked, and between 1876 and 1900 this infant branch of Orthodox Dissent grew impressively in membership by 61 per cent, and in numbers of congregations by 24 per cent.[31] Other bodies were stimulated by the Presbyterians' example. The General Baptists with their own denominational structures, finances, magazines, College, missionary society and local associations, had long been represented, indeed, considering their smallness, over-represented, in the conclaves of the Baptist Union. As a more liberalized church order spread among the Particular Baptists with the triumph of open communion principles, espoused by all the leading ministers and laymen of the day, and the sharper edges of Calvinism were smoothed away almost to vanishing point, there seemed little purpose in shunning the overtures of the smaller body, which was now identified in the public eye with Dr Clifford, the eloquent and active pastor of Praed Street Chapel, London. (Only a very few of the Particulars sensed just how theologically liberal the Generals had by now become.) The latter were of course proud of the family atmosphere of their little denomination, but their economic status was lowly, and recent events had demonstrated

---

[29] K. S. Inglis, *Churches and The Working Classes In Victorian England* (1963), 86f.
[30] R. Currie, *op cit*, 211.
[31] A. L. Macarthur, '1876 and the Unity of the Church' in *JPHS* xiii (4) (1967).

the advantages which would accrue from absorption into the larger body. They disbanded their organization in 1891, and threw in their lot with their senior brethren.

Some of the Methodist sects, smaller numerically than the General Baptists, were equally affected by unifying pressures. A great Methodist Ecumenical Conference held in 1881 had quickened the movement for unity, but the Primitives were a social problem, and among the Wesleyans, though the liberal wing led by Hughes and the prominent layman R. W. Perks in general favoured union, the conservative high churchmen did not. Eventually Bible Christians, New Connexionists and the United Free Methodists formally came together in 1907. This union was a triumph for a vaguely liberal theology, represented by William Redfern, and for the more highly organized and bureaucratic, yet smallest of the bodies, the Methodist New Connexion. Voting patterns in the denominational referenda were also most interesting: the churches in older established centres of denominational strength were usually against, newer suburban causes, especially in the Southeast where the very names UMFC or MNC bore an exotic air and embarrassed the young congregations which sported them, were far more favourable. 1907 thus established a pattern which has recurred in successive ecumenical enterprises down to the present day.

Most Nonconformists however set their sights on a wider union than any of these limited family reconciliations. As early as 1845 the Evangelical Alliance had endeavoured to bring about cooperation of a sort, but as it contained Anglicans, had only an individual membership and was rather shrill in its anti-Popery witness, it no longer provided a focus for the kind of unity felt desirable in the 1890s. A number of factors conspired to lower the denominational barriers in that particular decade. The world Methodist gathering of 1881 was followed by similar international conferences of Congregationals in 1891 and Baptists in 1905. The YMCA and Student Volunteer Missionary Union provided evidence of grass-roots cooperation. Home reunion conferences began to be held at Grindelwald in Switzerland in 1891, encouraged by H. S. Lunn, the Methodist tour operator; above all, a number of local Free Church Councils had been formed in major towns and cities, and provided a model of what was to follow nationally in 1896.[32] Yet the most significant ingredient in the Free Church Unity movement was undoubtedly the Wesleyan.

Here the organic and societary strain which had always been a basic presupposition emerged to the surface again in the so-called 'Christian Imperialism' of Hugh Price Hughes. This was a brash and vulgar affair, and, as formally launched in the *Methodist Times* in 1885, aimed to displace the Anglican Church, which these liberal Methodists particularly disliked, by a grand united Protestant federation, including

32 E. K. H. Jordan, *Free Church Unity* (1956), passim.

possibly Anglican Evangelicals. It was also hoped, and after the Parnell affair in 1889, with some justification, to capture the Liberal Party and use it as an instrument to discomfit the Conservatives, still regarded as the Established Church's political wing. Its apogee came with the Wesleyan Twentieth Century Fund of 1898 to build Westminster Central Hall across the road from Westminster Abbey as a sign to the world that the ascendency of the 'Anglican sect', as Hughes called it, was indeed at an end. Those Nonconformists who were also beginning to think in collectivist terms, such as Dr Clifford (though their inspiration was usually political and social rather than ecclesiastical) followed where Hughes led.

Older and wiser Dissenters, like the Congregationals Parker and Dale, retained their individualism to the end, and feared that collective political and ecclesiastical organizations and utterances of this kind would imperil the whole ethos of Nonconformity. They were not attended to. Great national Simultaneous Missions launched triumphantly in 1900 marked the beginning of the new century. But it was not to be long before ecumenicalism would be dimly apprehended, if not openly avowed, as the only check to diminishing resources and falling numbers.

2 Patterns of Belief

Changing creeds

Calvinism was softening among the Old Dissenters in the first two decades of the nineteenth century. A tough and logically consistent creed, it shrank in the works of the Congregationals Edward Williams (d. 1813) and J. Pye Smith (d. 1851) into '*Modified Calvinism*' or the '*New System*', a mixture of Calvinistic piety and the newer Arminian universalism. Despite what staunch Calvinists north and south of the border said about it, the New System had a respectable doctrinal ancestry stretching back through Thomas Scott and John Newton to Bunyan, Baxter and a fair number of the Puritan divines.

But outside the studies of the dissenting academies Moderate Calvinism was diffused into a cloudiness of doctrine, 'the sentiments usually denominated evangelical', as contemporaries put it, and the more dramatically rehearsed the preaching, the more heavily disguised the dogmatic inadequacy. Thus William Jay (1769–1853), one of the most distinguished Congregational preachers of the age, had, he believed, separated the 'inclusive' from the 'exclusive' in Calvinism and retained only the former, uniting it with the stirring exhortatory preaching of the Methodist revival which he greatly admired, taking an 'extended view' of the Puritan dogmatic heritage, employing it (in the simile of John Newton which was widely quoted in this period) as 'a lump of sugar to sweeten the tea'. But Jay never called himself a Calvinist at all—Calvinists he knew and admired, especially if a 'mild temper' had moderated their natural harshness, but they were other than he, and he approached them with some diffidence.[1] It is hard not to sympathize with R. W. Dale's sour description of the evangelicalism of this generation as 'Calvinism in decay'.

Baptists, with the Strict and Particulars quick to expose any deviation from perfect orthodoxy on the part of the mainstream churches, were bound to be more theologically conscious—and cautious, but when J. H. Hinton, their leading theologian endeavoured to accomplish a work similar to Edward Williams's he met with much less success. Hinton seemed to advocate both particular and general redemption

[1] J. H. Taylor, 'William Jay and his admirers' in *JURHS* i (3) (1974); The Autobiography of William Jay (reprinted, 1974).

at once, and though orthodox on many points exalted the sphere of human reason to a degree hitherto unknown among the Particular Baptists. Terribly contentious and wordy, he was at his serenest when, controversial divinity set aside, he could declaim in praise of the new style revivalism of the 1840s or of that Dissenting preoccupation of the mid-Victorian years, the domestic virtues, which Nonconformist households were believed to exemplify more satisfactorily than any others. Hinton's prominent role in the Baptist Union has concealed the idiosyncracies of his theological contribution. Thus while Congregationalism had a number of respectable intellectual mentors, the Particular Baptists had only the fading memory of the great Andrew Fuller or well-thumbed copies of Abraham Booth's moderate Calvinist classic, the *Reign of Grace*, written as long ago as 1768.

If the denominational trumpets gave an uncertain sound, it is hardly to be wondered at that the local churches were troubled with theological doubts and disputations. Church books reveal a number of interesting schisms—amongst the Baptists indeed whole groups of churches could secede to the Strict and Particulars in the 20s, 30s and 40s. Most of these were 'orthodox' revolts against a suspected unorthodox pastor—or even a slumbering, heretical but socially powerful chapel hierarchy—in which case the minister himself might well be among the schismatics. The carriages, Dr Binfield has observed, usually stayed with the old-established cause, the pony traps flocked to the secession.[2] Often, though, a transition to more liberal attitudes could be accomplished without too much controversy. Surrey Chapel, London, whose successive pastors were Rowland Hill, arch-Calvinist, James Sherman, moderate Calvinist and Newman Hall, loosely evangelical, revivalistic and advocate of 'the larger hope', that is a vague sort of universalism, is a case in point.

The factors which lie behind the decline of Calvinism are not easily identifiable. Arminian warmth was in the romantic age understandably more attractive than the intellectual rigours of Predestinationism; freewill may well have asserted itself in religious circles just because the prevailing secular philosophy, Utilitarianism, was so deterministic (though this is a double-edged argument for it could equally well be maintained that Calvinism should have been given a new lease of life by the all-pervading influence of philosophical necessarianism). Again, the sheer explosion of early nineteenth-century philanthropic concern may have underlined the improvability of the human lot and undermined fatalistic creeds of acceptance and submission; the ethical tradition of human responsibility, the Enlightenment's chief legacy to the succeeding age, may have proved increasingly irreconcilable with a theology of Divine Decrees. And on a more humdrum level the widespread abandonment by Nonconformist ministers of preaching through the Bible (in no instance did Spurgeon reveal himself the last of the

[2] C. Binfield, 'The Thread of Disruption' in *CHST* xx (5) (1967), 163.

Puritans more clearly than in this) led to a type of theologizing at once more eclectic and haphazard. Now Dissenting ministers would search the Scriptures for arresting texts ('the less observed and less improved portions of Scripture', as Jay called them), play wonderfully with words and phrases and turn out many a pithy axiom—but this was hardly doctrinal preaching. Indeed textual exposition and prophetic exhortation were now subsumed in 'experimentality', which most ministers took for granted was the only feasible type of preaching for the times in which they lived.

By the 1850s the type of evangelism which particularly emphasized personal experience appeared most attractive to the majority of thinking Dissenters who like Henry Allon cherished 'the responsibilities and prerogatives of the individual life'. Soon this individualism was to be fed powerfully by highly personalized Dissenting adaptations of Maurice and the Broadchurchmen's delicate Incarnationalism and the centring of religious idealism on the figure of the Christ Hero, Captain of Souls, Elder Brother, Comrade, Guide. Theological systematization was being denounced by the *Evangelical Magazine* and the *Eclectic Review* in the late 50s with vigour, almost with contempt. But the learned journals were behind the times: this was the unspoken position which the majority of Dissenting ministers, whether they called themselves Moderate Calvinists or not, had adopted soon after the great revulsion against 'Antinomian' excesses in the 1800s. By mid-century, as Silvester Horne was to remark, no churchmen had become so permeated with Broadchurch principles as Freechurchmen, and by 1891 D. W. Simon could report to the International Congregational Council that over the past twenty-five years hardly any theological and even fewer doctrinal works had appeared from the pens of Congregational divines.

Biblical theory was yielding to experience: 'systems of doctrine are trifles light as air to souls that see God face to face in immediate fellowship with the Eternal Spirit', wrote Dr Clifford in 1888.[3] Harnack, Ritschl and Sabatier, siren voices calling from the Continent, were to underline this subjectivism. Theology had also yielded to religion reinterpreted as progress. Dr W. F. Adeney, a powerful voice in Congregationalism in the 90s, saw religious belief in Darwinian terms as developing simultaneously with the social and political progress of the natural world.[4] Needless to say Nonconformity, no longer defended by an appeal to apostolic precedent, but to its opposite, a prophetic guess as to what the future might legitimate, marked the highest form of religious progress to date. Particularly clever divines like A. M. Fairbairn, another Congregational, could even reinterpret such progress in Hegelian terms to the admiration of their less gifted flocks.

Hegel, at second or third hand, no doubt accounts also for the

[3] J. Marchant, *Dr John Clifford* (1924), 31.
[4] W. F. Adeney, *A Century's Progress* (1901).

widespread immanentism, assuming in extreme cases, like the Congregational J. B. Snell, pantheistic forms, which flourished in the last decades of the century. Even in the 1860s, J. Baldwin Brown, also a Congregational, had evolved his own peculiar brand of religionless Christianity. Soon afterwards, theological paraphrases of Browning and Carlyle's naturalistic supernaturalism had become the stock-in-trade of Nonconformist preachers, and by the 90s widespread immanentism had led to a general depreciation of the sacraments, discipline and church order. Free souls, having encapsulated God within themselves, surveyed majestically a world ripe for Utopian experiment.

The Church was finally reduced, as Clifford put it, into 'a social engine whose exclusive and explicit aim it is to actualize the kingdom.' Likewise any movement of progressives such as the Labour Party was itself a Church, ushering in the same dream-kingdom of ethical aspiration.

Church and society, kingdom of God and kingdom of man, were by now hopelessly confused, especially in the thought of R. J. Campbell, Congregational promoter of The New Theology movement (1907). The very term 'Church' was in fact vanishing in Nonconformist circles in the 1890s, 'ecclesia' or 'brotherhood' being preferred. 'A self-governing fraternity where all were free and equal' was Pierce and Horne's definition of the Church in their (Congregational) *Manual of Church Fellowship* (1893). The folly of such debasement of the church idea was appreciated by very few, though a handful among the Congregationals saw correctly that a Social Gospel cut off completely from the historic Christian past was no gospel at all, merely a restatement of Law.[5] Elsewhere the new evangelism, as it was sometimes called, carried everything before it. Something of its headiness is still communicated by a reading of Dr Clifford's Fabian Tracts: Garett Horder's popular hymnal, *Worship Song* (1905) stands as its most bizarre memorial.[6]

Traditional church order was clearly floundering in much the same way as traditional doctrine. The church covenant, the foundation deed of Independent Churches, was now seen to be cast in an uncomfortably Calvinistic mould and so was set aside or conveniently forgotten. (But the evidence of past times handled in a highly selective and outrageous manner could be of help to some advanced ministers. The fact that Independents and Presbyterians in the wholly orthodox atmosphere of the post-1662 era had attended one another's ordinations was in the 80s and 90s used as an excuse on the part of Congregationals to take part in Unitarian ordinations in ex-Presbyterian chapels!)

[5] J. W. Grant, *Freechurchmanship In England*, 1870–1940 (n.d.), 184.
[6] Such 'progressiveness' may be viewed as a belated catching up on the part of bewildered middle-class churches with the enormous physical and psychological changes implicit in Victorian urban and particularly suburban life-styles. An explanation this may be, but hardly an excuse: see J. H. S. Kent, 'The Role of Religion in the Cultural Structure of the Later Victorian City' in *TRHS* 5th series, xxiii (1973).

The concept of the church as a fellowship of believers united as a theocracy against the world yielded to the belief that by stressing their democratic character and their historic contribution to secular democracy the churches would put themselves in harmony with the times. As J. W. Grant puts it, 'Nonconformists were beginning to accept as part of their church doctrine the secular forms of their own beliefs. Political ideas coloured the religious philosophy from which they had sprung.'[7]

Within the individual congregations this change of emphasis often took the form of an assertion of the rights of the people to support or oppose the minister (or diaconate) as they pleased, not, as tradition demanded, of their collective duty to oppose the Crown Rights of the Redeemer against the pressures of a hostile world. Yet paradoxically these 'democratic clubs', as J. G. Rogers described the palsied Independency of his own day, allowed the most significant expression of their ecclesiastical democracy, the Church Meeting, to fall into decay.[8] As the Churches became increasingly departmentalized after the 1830s, so the Church Meeting degenerated into a body where occasional trials of strength interrupted trifling debates on bazaars, magazines, raffles and eventually pantomimes. It certainly no longer dealt with what had been its most vital concern at the start of the century, that concern highlighted by Mark Rutherford in his novels, the admission of new members and the disciplining of the wayward. Obligatory public testimony was regarded by the 1840s as an infringement of personal rights; discipline, though it lasted into the 60s and 70s, in cases of moral lapse and bankruptcy, wore an increasingly old-fashioned and repressive air. When, particularly in the towns, a popular preacher drew vast and often ephemeral congregations, not one half of whom wished to take up membership, but many of whom claimed the right of attending communion without actually being on the church roll, polity and discipline alike suffered. But the 'Rev. Erasmus Newlight LLB' arguing with the 'Rev. Elias Oldways' in the *Eclectic Review* for 1868 found such laxity and freedom from ecclesiastical restraint 'very beautiful'.

Much of this decay is to be explained by over-reaction to the Tractarian movement in the 30s and 40s. Even the decline of the church idea, the Puritan concept of the congregation as a sacerdotal society, a kingdom of priests, may be explained in this way. The Tractarians' exaltation of the sacraments led Dissenters either to neglect them altogether, to tack them on to the end of the preaching service, or to insist on lay administration as a counter to priestly claims. Among Baptists highly individualistic ideas concerning their peculiar rite developed within the same context. It was the ministry which suffered the most however, not in respect of career prospects, for despite vast differences in stipends, the Nonconformist ministry remained, as

[7] J. W. Grant, *op. cit.*, 112.
[8] See J. H. Taylor, 'The Survival of the Church Meeting' in *CHST* xxi (2) (1971).

George Eliot observed, the best means for a talented youth of lowly origins to 'get on', but certainly in respect of the dignity of office. Ordination fell victim to a 'recognition' or even a 'welcoming' service,[9] the title Reverend was abjured, clerical dress, gown and bands, disappears among the young men of Newlight's generation, the growing of beards and moustaches marks his emancipation from the clerical caste. The ministry was now interpreted like any other profession in terms of wordly success, character and abilities were stressed at the expense of the dignity of the office. In this atmosphere ministerial casualties abounded—bruised ex-ministers delighted the world with accounts of their sufferings at the hands of persecuting flocks.

But as long as the spirit of the age bore the churches confidently in the direction of limitless progress, these democratizing tendencies[10] were accepted as inevitable, and indeed desirable. Having surrendered so much, it is not surprising that in the early 90s the most vital element of all should have been jettisoned, the idea of the gathered church itself. Till about 1892 the concessions of the Anglican scholar Edwin Hatch, who in his Bampton Lectures of 1880 had seemed to admit the apostolic character of ecclesiastical democracy, an appreciation among the learned of the arguments of the German theologian Alfred Harnack and a supposed early dating of the ancient Christian text known as the Didache had convinced Nonconformists scholars that the only form of polity to be found in the New Testament was that of the gathered church. With surprising suddenness it was by 1895 conceded that Scripture revealed a range of evolving church structures, and that different ecclesiologies could be held with equal conviction. 'The time has gone by when any order of churches can flourish simply by its polity', declared the Congregational Union in that year, 'it must prove its adaptability to the wants of the age'. But by this time ecclesiasticism of any kind had grown so unpopular that not even so startling a shift attracted very much notice.

Doctrine faltered, church order decayed, and beginning in the 1840s, and with accelerating speed after 1880, Nonconformist scholars began to yield to the conclusions of the biblical higher critics and to question the bedrock of their faith, the Inerrancy of Sacred Scripture.[11] But their achievement in the field of biblical scholarship could only be tentative and defensive. Having few scholars of eminence themselves (largely because of the University Tests which still hamstrung them), they at first took shelter behind the Anglican trio of New Testament critics, Westcott, Lightfoot and Hort, and in particular Edwin Hatch, a biblical scholar as well as a church historian. Secondly, they fell back upon the archaeologists, especially the conservative A. H. Sayce,

[9] J. H. Taylor, 'Ordination Among Us' in *CHST* xx (7) (1965).
[10] P. T. Forsyth preferred the terms 'anabaptist' or 'spirtualizing', but these had special meanings for this great scholar, not immediately obvious to others.
[11] W. B. Glover, *Evangelical Nonconformists and Higher Criticism in the Nineteenth Century* (1954), 71f.

in the hope that this most tangible of disciplines might refute the more extreme critics. Thirdly, they trusted that if their proclamation of the traditional evangelical certainties was sufficiently loud and clear, critical considerations could be somehow stifled or ignored, a tactic employed, perhaps unwittingly, by preachers as great as Alexander McLaren, the Demosthenes of the Manchester Baptists. Fourthly, they could betake themselves to what J.M. Gibbon defined as *Evangelical Heterodoxy*,[12] the uttering of warm evangelical sentiments and a continued use of evangelical language, while imparting to their words meanings totally different from, indeed abhorrent to, those common to Evangelicals of a former era. Of this dubious art also Fairbairn was a past master and his imitators numerous.

Finally, ministers could on grounds of prudence conceal from their flocks the direction in which their intellectual discoveries were leading them. Many later Victorian divines preferred preaching to writing, where their unorthodoxies would be more easily detected, and made no secret of the fact that the insights they could share with the scholars they dared not divulge to their traditionalist flocks. Robertson Nichol in fact edited both *The Expositor*, the most outstanding journal of biblical criticism in England in the 90s, and a sign that Nonconformist scholarship was at last beginning to escape from Anglican tutelage, and *The British Weekly*, a popular religious journal. The latter organ was conservative and orthodox, with no more than an occasional hint of the revolution proceeding apace in the theological colleges.

Inevitably each denomination in turn was involved in controversy when newer insights clashed with accepted modes of presentation and understanding, which survived with particular tenacity in provincial England.

Congregationalism was first disturbed by the enforced resignation of the liberal W. B. Clulow from his lectureship at Airedale College in 1843, and then by the publication of Edward White's *Life of Christ* (1846), a book which transmuted the idea of eternal punishment into conditional immortality or 'the larger hope'. It aroused controversy at the time, yet by the 1880s liberal insights had spread so rapidly in the denomination that leading divines were confident that the yet more radical doctrine of universal restoration, the ultimate salvation of all men, was far more in tune with the times than the painless extinction of the wicked. (Conditionalists like White and Universalists like Baldwin Brown vied with one another in their anxiety to be 'contemporary'. Despite their differences they both agreed that Benthamite theories of punishment, Darwinian biology and the various ideas of progress all rendered the traditional Christian eschatology, especially the doctrine of Hell, obnoxious and untenable[13].)

[12] J. M. Gibbon, *Evangelical Heterodoxy* (1909).
[13] See further G. Rowell, *Hell and The Victorians* (1974), a work which is splendid on changes in Anglican thought, less happy in its treatment of Nonconformity.

The Rivulet Controversy of 1855 which arose over the publication by the Reverend T. T. Lynch of a hymnal containing verses of a simplistic, nature-worshipping character, could have been more damaging than the argument over White's book, but was somehow diverted into a quarrel over the editorial responsibility of Dr Campbell, one of Lynch's critics and the 'Congregational Press Baron' of the times, *vis à vis* the Congregational Union. The Samuel Davidson case of 1856 was more serious still. Davidson was a tutor at the Lancashire Independent College, Manchester, and though on the surface his offence was a fairly advanced biblical criticism, it was, underneath, his liberal theology and at a still deeper level his failure to conceal his stark opinions under a cloud of envangelical sentiment which led to his dismissal from his chair. That his defeat was really a Pyrrhic victory for his conservative opponents was shown by Henry Allon's declaring only eight years later that biblical inerrancy was now doomed in the denomination.

How rapidly the liberal tide was carrying Congregationals was again demonstrated in 1877 at the Leicester Conference when J. A. Picton, at the head of a group of advanced ministers, boldly redefined the Christian religion as feeling (and feeling of the vaguest kind) and denounced confessionalism of any variety. This time the conservatives were truly alarmed and reacted vigorously, and a small, and now forgotten, school of traditionalist scholarship led by Alfred Cave and John Kennedy arose in the denomination. It was to no avail. Congregationals, lay and clerical alike, were proud of being in the forefront of scholarship, and touchy about their hard-won social prestige—heresy hunts were intolerable in so enlightened a body. At the very time Spurgeon was making his stand over the Baptist Downgrade in 1888, Alexander Mackennal gave authoritative guidance to the Congregational denomination by drawing a sharp distinction between evolving doctrine (universally acceptable) and static dogma (totally abhorrent). His pronouncement drew widespread applause.

There were limits however, even in the most liberal of the so called orthodox denominations of Protestant Dissent. When the following year R. F. Horton published his *Inspiration Of The Bible*, a particularly negative and destructive work, the reaction was sufficient to provoke him into providing a 'constructive' sequel the following year. But the way was now prepared, through the radicalizing influences of Westhill College, Birmingham, and of the Mansfield College, Oxford, summer schools, for R. J. Campbell's *New Theology*, the most egregious expression of secular optimism wrapped in a glittering sheen of theological obfuscation yet inflicted on English Christendom.

Congregational controversies occasioned minor disturbances, were spread over a long period of time, and are scarcely remembered today. The Baptists paraded their divisions on one significant occasion only, a crucial struggle of principle whose memory periodically returns to haunt the denomination.[14] By the 1880s the traditionalism of the Baptists was under attack from several quarters—from the distinguished scholar, Dr Samuel Cox, removed from the editorial board of the *Expositor* in 1884 for advanced thoughts on the 'larger hope' and other problems, from Rawdon College whose principal from 1863–76 had been S. G. Green, a teacher of singularly advanced views, from the gradual permeation into the local churches of liberal insights under the guise of a liberalised, open-communion, open-membership polity, from the influence exerted in certain areas by General Baptists whose Old Connexion was now fully Unitarian and whose New was well on the way to becoming so. (Spurgeon was explicitly to disclaim that his quarrel was with the Arminian Baptists, but the fact that as early as the 1860s the General Baptists had been condemning Calvinism by appeals to the Unitarian Channing, and that John Clifford's disdain for theological forms was notorious, made their liberalism a significant background factor in the Downgrade Controversy).

In 1887 Charles Haddon Spurgeon, backed by his vast lower-middle class following in south London, threw down the gauntlet to the denominational leaders by linking higher critical views with theological declension, that suspect conflation which most Nonconformist divines were at pains to avoid, and by pointing out that 'it is mere cant to cry, We are all Evangelicals, We are all Evangelicals, and yet decline to say what Evangelical means.'

Confronted by a now omnipotent denominational hierarchy determined that the boat should not be rocked, and holding in its grip individual churches which could no longer afford the luxury of secession, Spurgeon encountered from his fellow ministers subterfuge, silence or sullen hostility, and on the part of the Baptist Union a determination to accommodate him no further than by issuing the vaguely evangelical Declaratory Statement of 1888. Spurgeon, having failed in his plea for a voluntary return to the Old Faith, fell back, like John Keble in the Gorham crisis of 1850, on to the piety and principles of his own local church: if the Baptists should fail nationally, their historic distinctiveness would still be found at the Metropolitan Tabernacle. Spurgeon and his church left the Union, the grandest gesture yet against the debilitating forces at work within English Nonconformity.

The Presbyterian Church of England was troubled in the wake of the Downgrade Controversy. A production called the *Articles of Faith* (1888) sought to tone down the rigidities of the Westminster Confession, but immediately there set in a conservative backlash, partly clerical but partly lay-inspired, which four years later resulted in an uneasy doctrinal compromise but was also strong enough to prevent the

[14] The fullest account of the Down-grade Controversy is to be found in a paper deposited by Dr E. A. Payne in the Library of the Baptist Union. But see also his *Baptist Union, A Short History* (1959), 124f.

radical George Adam Smith being elected to a vacant chair at West-minster Theological College. Among Presbyterians a strong tradi-tionalist element, drawing its strength from north of the border, prevented the kind of frenzied descent into nothingarianism on which much of English Dissent was now plainly embarked.[15]

Above the storms of critical controversy the Wesleyan body stood majestically, convinced that its evangelical Arminianism and holiness ethic, its renowned discipline modified by timely concession, would preserve the connexion from the ravages of the scholars. Wesleyanism's submission came in consequence late, following on a phase of grudging surrenders, each one accompanied by an official lecture whose 'thus far and no farther' theme grew wearisomely familiar.

As late as 1870 the *London Quarterly Review*, reviewing Cheyne's new *Commentary on Jeremiah*, remarked that though his writings belonged to the 'semi-destructive school', yet, considering the vastness of his learning and his sincerity, Wesleyans should take 'an interest in him, an interest filled with hope'. It was, however, the Wesleyans and not the Professor who were shortly to be converted. In 1887 the Reverend Dr Dallinger's Fernley Lecture, which had accepted the evolutionary viewpoint but which he had for seven years been discouraged from publishing, was at last given the connexional imprimatur. Henceforth evolutionary science was officially accepted, and doctrine fell into the background, though it is symptomatic of Wesleyan conservatism that as late as 1898 and again in 1902 the Reverend J. Agar Beet was censured by Con-ference for unorthodox ideas of hell.

By the 90s under the leadership of younger progressive scholars such as M. G. Pearse, Scott Lidgett and W. T. Davison, Wesleyan theology approximated more closely to that of the more liberal denominations. The *Recorder* and the *Methodist Times* were in the forefront of advance, the *Wesleyan Methodist Magazine* and the *London Quarterly Review* clinging more obstinately to the older theology. Their witness was to little purpose, for towering over the entire Wesleyan scene was now the tragi-comic figure of Hugh Price Hughes, a keen Evangelical and Tory in his student days at Richmond College, but thereafter theologically advanced, 'accommodating' in his peculiarly hectoring way, and a political Liberal, much concerned for social purity and an aggressive sort of teetotalism. Few other ministerial careers reveal how far Wesleyanism had travelled in the century of progress: even his youthful conversion the elder Hughes felt constrained to describe as his 'illumination'.[16]

In the Methodist sects the pull of tradition was far less strong than in the parent body. The New Connexion had always prided itself on its 'rational' and 'temperate' doctrines and Free Methodism on its free thought, as well as its democratic polity, yet it was among the Primitives

[15] W. B. Glover, *op. cit.*, 196f.
[16] D. P. Hughes, *The Life of Hugh Price Hughes* (1904), 20.

where A. S. Peake was appointed to Hartley College in 1892 that Evangelical Arminianism was being most rapidly transformed into universal benevolence, while critical views and advanced political posturings became endemic among the younger men. The forms of traditional piety remained, the substance was transformed out of recognition. Dr Currie's description of the state of Christological thought in later nineteenth-century Methodism is both cruel and just, and has reference to a much wider Nonconformist constituency. 'Christ was now like a popular minister of religion, smiling but grave, enormously learned, wise and experienced, but full of help, understanding, generosity and fun ... Religion was a permanent Sunday School Anniversary, Christ the affable minister, the universe a tidy church hall full of happy faces.'[17] A spiritualized version of Blatchford's Merrie England was the best that most Nonconformist leaders could by now offer their still vast but slowly diminishing congregations.

The revival factor

Delightful heresy of all kinds might entrance the Dissenting clergy and the educated laity, and might through their agency percolate down to the rest. In most Nonconformist communities, however, it was revival which was the perennial and all-absorbing concern throughout the entire century.

Religious revivalism was still in 1800 unstructured, spontaneous and eagerly awaited as a gracious outpouring of God's spirit, 'a shower of blessing', whose only human predeterminant was intensive and prolonged prayer on the part of penitent churchmen that a revival would be in fact vouchsafed. This kind of 'awakening', which had swept America and England in the eighteenth century, was still occurring in the 1810s and 1820s and well beyond. Primitive Methodism, largely a rural movement, the hyper-emotional side of the 'revolt of the field', certainly falls into this category, as do the 'tent meeting' revivals on vacant plots in town suburbs, from which in the 20s a new denomination, the Tent Methodists, emerged. Till late in the century in remote areas like Cornwall, and especially in religious communities where the working class predominated, revival could occur, spontaneously under lay leadership, often to the embarrassment of ministers. The Welsh revival of 1904 partakes somewhat of this character.

Much has been written recently as to the economic circumstances favouring or discouraging movements of revival, Hobsbawm, Thompson and Currie insisting that revivals flourish after political and economic aspirations have met with defeat, others pointing out that religious and political excitement often accompany one another in time and

[17] R. Currie, *op. cit.*, 125.

place (notable Methodist revivals occurred in the stress years 1832–34, 1838–40 and 1848–50), that economic distress often aided revivalism as in the Lancashire Cotton Famine, that booms, on the contrary, could produce religious depression, and that the mental unsettlement occasioned by cholera and other epidemics may well have been a more powerful fillip to revival than political excitement in the metropolis and the great towns.[18]

What has chiefly concerned historians however has not been the causative factors underlying revivals but the changing techniques of the revivalists themselves, their growing professionalism as opposed to the spontaneity of the earlier awakenings. Dr Kent has seen the publication of the Reverend C. Colton's *History and Character of American Revivals of Religion* (1832) as a turning point.[19] Here at last the 'promotion of revivals' was geared to 'human instrumentality', 'systematic effort', 'human calculation by the arithmetic of faith in God's arrangements.' Whether behind this lies the supersession of Calvinism by Arminianism, of classical Protestantism by a more humanistic philosophy, or simply the realization that highly organized revivals were in a secularized society a convenient means of keeping the children loyal and out of temptation must be matters of contention.

So too must the precise role of Charles Finney, the American revivalist, in this movement towards professionalism. Dr Kent believes that Finney exaggerated his own standing as the herald of the 'new' revivalism, and that there was a native English professional revivalism which had been growing up before Finney's first visit to these Isles in 1849. But certainly Finney contributed to the new revivalism its lay and anti-clerical stance, its deliberate cultivation of 'old time religion' as a kind of folk movement opposed to parsonical dryness and rigidity.

What is not in dispute is that from the 1840s onwards revivals were being arranged in advance, halls booked, posters printed, the 'anxious seat' and 'protracted meeting' duly provided and advertised, and a whole range of intensely powerful and sometimes dubious techniques of persuasion (the false penitent for example) were being directed towards limited groups of persons, often adherents or Sunday School scholars or members of societies peripheral to the life of the local church, who were the prearranged targets of the revivalists' endeavours.

The new revivalism reached its climax in the Second Evangelical Awakening of 1859–65. The extent of this revival is hotly disputed. To Dr Kent it was a non-starter; what the churches saw happening was apparently an exercise in self-deception, the revivalists' efforts served only to underline the gap between middle-class churches and an

[18] E. J. Hobsbawm, 'Methodism and the Threat of Revolution in Britain' in *Labouring Men* (paperback edn. 1968), 32; E. P. Thompson, *The Making of The English Working Class* (1963), 389–91; R. Currie, *op. cit.*, 90f; R. B. Walker, 'The Growth of Wesleyan Methodism in England and Wales' in *J Ecc H* xxiv (1973).
[19] J. H. S. Kent, *American Revivalism and England in the Nineteenth Century* (Past and Present Conference Papers, 1966).

alienated proletariat. But at the time commentators thought differently.[20] Though there were enormous geographical variations, and
though the gap between the alleged count of converts and actual
accessions of new members was considerable, some denominations,
especially the Baptists, experienced a golden decade in the 60s, the
Wesleyans recovered after the depression of the 50s, and the Methodist
sects took on a new lease of life. (For some in fact the revival brought
salvation from total eclipse. The United Methodist Free Churches
were before 1860 fighting for their survival, and the New Connexion in
many areas was disappearing altogether.)

Historians are becoming slowly conscious, moreover, that it was in
these years that Nonconformity made an heroic and not unsuccessful
effort to establish itself in an urban setting, to strike roots deep enough
to secure it a significant place in the evolving self-consciousness of the
urban masses. The example of the Primitive Methodists in the 60s, 70s
and 80s reveals that the more countryside-based a denomination had
been in the past, the more challenging and exhilarating was the
attempted conquest of the towns, once revival in an urban setting had
become a possibility.

What is less in dispute are two other features of the Second Awakening, the heightened degree of professionalism among the revivalists, and
the renewed impulse given to a further withdrawal of a large segment
of lay Dissenters from those social and political concerns which had
come to characterize organized Nonconformity in the popular
mind. The professionalism showed itself in the curious class distinctions
which began to emerge in the course of the awakening. Revivalists
exhorted and converted men of their own sort in the manner most
appropriate to their conditions: Fiddler Joss Poole enjoyed success
among the roughs, Lord Radstock, the converted nobleman, among his
fellow peers, Henry Varley, a Baptist butcher, amongst tradespeople.
Soon even more distinguished revivalists with a marked penchant for
different occupational groups came onto the scene: Richard Weaver
for the lower orders, Reginald Ratcliffe for businessmen, Brownlow
North for the professional classes.

For the retreat into an introspective holiness spirituality, into group
soul-surgery and into what must strike outsiders as other-worldly
sectarianism, two influential books, William Arthur's *Tongue of Fire*
(1856) and T. Upham's *Life of Faith* (1859) plus the agonizingly
personal testimony of the revivalists were chiefly responsible. Here the
influence of women, particularly prominent in the 1860s can not be
overlooked.[21] The uncultured Amazons of the Primitive Methodist
revival, Elizabeth Bultitude and company, had given place in the 50s
to more highly trained cadres of female workers in Nonconformist
churches, bible women, scripture readers, visitors, class leaders,

[20] See too J. E. Orr, *The Second Evangelical Awakening In Britain* (1949), *passim*.
[21] O. Anderson, 'Women Preachers in Mid-Victorian Britain' in *CHJ* xii (3), (1969).

deaconesses. But reacting, albeit unconsciously, against this female activism arose the women preachers of the Second Awakening, upper-class ladies addressing lowly audiences, deeply spiritual and profoundly influenced by Brethrenite and holiness teaching, opposed to secular feminism and emphasizing a premillenial eschatology, the separation of small companies of believers from a darkening world to await the Last Days in solemn and pious seclusion.

The advent in 1875 of Moody and Sankey with their techniques of mass evangelism might have caused Nonconformity to lurch yet more decisively in the direction of a world-renouncing pietism, yet its effects were far otherwise. Moody's achievement, most marked in that adherents, fringe supporters usually of the lower middle classes, were now brought into closer connection with the churches whose memberships for a decade or so showed impressive increases, reinforced Nonconformity's urban success. The secular, non-clerical atmosphere of the Halls and Tabernacles which now proliferated, the reassuring combination of heartfelt preaching, ethical simplicities and wistful song provided a type of warm fellowship which had till then been largely lacking in towns and cities alike. A popular chord was struck—theological niceties were lacking, hell fire unmentioned, yet God was shown to be wonderfully active in the commonplaces of life. (Torrey and Alexander in the new century were to be theologically even vaguer, yet hotter, more intense, and with perhaps a note of desperation absent in their American forerunners.) The simple charm (or bathos) of the Moody-Sankey appearances wrought in their audiences surprisingly thorough and long-lasting commitments: somehow they elicited from the respectable town-dwellers whom they touched the last upsurge of the older evangelical belief that individual conversion demands a life-style where personal evangelism vies with a zeal for good works.

A similar result was seen in the most powerful of the agencies which arose in the wake of the mission, the Salvation Army. The real purport of *In Darkest England and The Way Out*, the movement's most notorious blueprint for a reformed society, has been hotly debated. The book has been seen by some as a shift to social emphases after a phase of disillusionment with a purely conversionist approach, by others as a kind of Nonconformist Young England, a terrifyingly authoritarian restatement of older societary values against the current individualism, and, more recently, as a way of resolving internal difficulties within the Army, particularly the waning of popular support and discontent among the officers. Whatever interpretation is placed upon General Booth's motivation however, few can dispute that the Salvation Army shared with the Moody and Sankey revival a phenomenal record of success (after only three years of existence its total of attendances exceeded those of the Primitive Methodists and were three quarters of the Baptists'), possessed a largely lower middle-class membership (after the initial outburst when it recruited from the rootless and unstable of

all classes), and went in for a marked avoidance of theological specula-
tion (once premillenialism and faith-healing had both been put down
by fiat).[22]

Once again pietistic withdrawal, an emphasis on the 'exceeding
sinfulness of sin', an individual asceticism and perfectionism and
general indifference to politics and social agitation was sanely balanced by a passionate concern for the outcast and downcast which has
characterized the Army ever since. 'We', said Booth in 1880 with
pardonable pride, 'are the moral scavengers, netting the very sewers.'
Not for the first time English popular religion, traditionalist and
unsophisticated but far from being the opiate or social discipline
which Leftist historians imagine, had proved that it had a life of its
own, was capable of spiritual discernment, and could produce generous
and realistic responses to contemporary social needs.

As time wore on, however, tension between the world-renouncing
and world-affirming elements in popular Nonconformity, adumbrated
in the Second Awakening, was bound to become more obvious and
intense. Beginning as a movement of the sophisticated and fashionable,
a new pietism rapidly spread through the length and breadth of
Nonconformity. The motives of those who embraced it may have been
shrewdly human as well as religious, for as Robert Moore has shown
from his examination of four closely-knit Durham mining villages at
the end of the century,[23] the retreat to pietism was aided by the
deliberate decision to exclude from the chapel community's purview
divisive issues such as Socialist politics which would shatter its unity.
But whatever the explanation the retreat was very real, and its symbol
rapidly became the Keswick Convention.

The Conventions which combined holiness concern with personal
evangelism were for their first fifteen years dominated by Evangelical
Anglicans, but in the 1890s there was a marked influx of Nonconformists. (Local Conventions which sprang up in imitation of Keswick were
often Nonconformist in character from the very start.) The Convention
movement was not anti-intellectual and possessed a deep missionary
concern. Nor was it wholly middle class, though Spurgeon poured scorn
on it for just this reason.[24] Some of its most earnest Nonconformist
promoters like the Baptist minister F. B. Meyer managed moreover
to reconcile its pietistic impulses with an active social concern, in his
particular case the moral purity crusade. Yet it is hard to avoid the
conclusion that the Convention movement took increasing numbers of
Nonconformists out of the world (possibly in the long run for their own
good, for it is world-renouncing Nonconformity which enjoys the

---

[22] See R. Robertson, 'The Salvation Army' in B. R. Wilson (ed.), *Patterns of
Sectarianism* (1967); K. S. Inglis, *op. cit.*, 175f.
[23] R. Moore, *Pitmen, Preachers and Politics* (1974), 58f.
[24] C. Binfield, *George Williams and The YMCA* (1973) is very useful for the Non-
conformist/Anglican background to 'Keswick'.

greatest staying power). Dissenters retreated in hopefulness or desperation from the struggle and bustle of political and social conflict to the inward repose of holiness Christianity.

George Adam Smith observed at the time that while the Moody-Sankey missions led to a heightening of philanthropic zeal on the one hand, on the other they led a large proportion of the middle-class to spend their leisure time running from Convention to Convention, feeling that this was the highest duty and happiest privilege of the Christian calling. It was the 1890s however which saw 'Keswickism' reinforced by the rapid spread of Brethren assemblies and undenominational mission halls, and Nonconformists in considerable numbers experiencing a gut-reaction against the type of abrasive Dissent which had helped them in their quest for self-improvement and status in the past in favour of something altogether quieter, a simple pietism they could share with the Evengelical Anglicans whom they greatly admired and with whom they longed to be at peace. (It is a fact not recorded in the textbooks that Nonconformists who were associated with the Convention movement were either completely indifferent to the Balfour Education Act of 1902 or else sympathized openly with the Anglican Evangelical standpoint.)

If leaders as great as Dale and Parker were shunning party politics as divisive, fearing the transformation of the Dissenting churches into 'politico-religious debating clubs', or the shattering effect of the emergence of a separate Nonconformist Party, it is hardly to be wondered at that lesser men should take the opportunity to opt out altogether. The sound and fury of the Passive Resistance League of 1902–06 was the work of a few ministerial and lay *enragés*, significant only because by then they were so exceptional. Wise Dissenters were cultivating the spirit.

3 Patterns of Activity

Sunday Schools and missions

One of the more searching criticisms which Dr R. W. Dale made of the impact of the Evangelical revival was that it reduced the classical doctrine of justification into a persuasive to ethical endeavour, a release from the Law which itself became a legalistic category, a gigantic moral 'work'.[1] Justification by works was indeed the cry raised by old-fashioned Nonconformists, especially those of the Calvinistic sort, when about 1800 the cohesiveness of the individual gathered church began to be stretched and then broken by the first of those subordinate, all-engaging and time-consuming institutions which in the words of Guiness Rogers, one of Dale's Congregational contemporaries, were increasingly to 'clutter up' the churches' life as the century progressed.[2]

The Sunday School movement was the child of the revival. In the 1790s it had been largely undenominational in spirit, and vast buildings of which that at Stockport was the most famous had been supported by the whole gamut of denominations from Roman Catholics to Unitarians to cope with the massive increase in the juvenile population which characterized those years. But the French Revolution had shattered the undenominational ideal, Anglicans grew fearful of the imagined challenge to the Establishment principle which the schools posed, and in their panic allowed the Dissenters, especially the Wesleyans, to step into the role they seemed only too anxious to vacate. By 1800 the Sunday School attached to the local congregation, sometimes very closely and on the same premises, sometimes more loosely and in its own purpose-built rooms, was becoming the Dissenting norm.

From the very first Nonconformists were both to value the benefits and sense the dangers of the Sunday School movement. Its chief merit, as Professor Ward reminds us, was that it stood out as 'the only religious institution which the nineteenth-century public in the mass had any intention of using'.[3] It taught the children of poor parents

---

[1] R. W. Dale, *The Evangelical Revival and Other Sermons* (1880); *The Laws of Christ For Common Life* (1884), 34f.
[2] Quoted by Rogers' son, Stanley Rogers, in his *After Forty Years* (1918), 29.
[3] See further W. R. Ward, *Religion and Society*, 135f.

how to read, in some cases how to write, it was a useful training ground for life and inculcated sound moral principles, it provided simple entertainments and its outings could be among the highlights of the local community's year. And from the churches' point of view it constituted the most obvious recruiting ground for new members from the unchurched masses. (Just how effective a recruiting ground was the object of some statistical heart-searching in Dissenting circles later on in the century.)

The dangers were more subtle: the Sunday School could easily become a state within a state, with a life and ethos of its own, separate from the parent church, their orbits meeting only once a year on the occasion of the Anniversary, or 'Sermons' as they were known in the North, the church officers and even the minister excluded from its weekly sessions. Again, as the Sunday School children were of lowly social position (their occasional presence in church, the aristocratic Dr Martineau once remarked, was made known to him in the pulpit by four out of his five senses[4]), the offspring of respectable church members were often discouraged from attending the institution themselves, had perforce to accompany their parents to the adult services, grew bored, and fell away in adulthood. Sometimes the Sunday School was so independent that it became the nucleus of a new church (a fact which at least in theory fitted in with the Independent idea of spontaneous growth as the prerequisite of successful church extension); later on it could become theologically and politically wayward, and links with the mother church could be snapped amid reproaches and controversy.[5]

The Wesleyans felt these dilemmas acutely. Recruiting such vast numbers of children in the first two decades of the century that they had the human material to become the alternative Church of town and countryside alike, Bunting and his party shrank from the outlay in men and materials involved in such an enterprise. In the 1820s when the schools were suspected of republicanism, failing to raise up enough converts, providing a disincentive to the children of members to join the church, and being subversive of the class system, a deliberate campaign was launched to end the dangerous practice of teaching writing, to cultivate quality rather than quantity and to bring the schools more firmly under ministerial control. The result of Bunting's Conference legislation was that in all the Methodist secessions the Sunday School factor is to be found lurking in the background, in the Warrenite revolt where entire schools went over in some places and Associationist churches were formed out of them, and in the 1849 troubles when Everett, the most popular of Sunday School Anniversary preachers, attracted a good many teachers and their schools to the

---

[4] James Martineau, quoted in H. D. Roberts, *Hope Street Church* (1909), 355.
[5] R. Moore provides a very interesting example of such wayward behaviour in the socialistic Primitive Methodist bible class of Quebec village, Co. Durham,—Moore, *op. cit.*, 170f.

Wesleyan Reformers' cause. Once the blood-letting was over, it became Conference policy to allow the Sunday School a free hand in matters indifferent, while subtly expanding the Wesleyan machinery to subordinate the schools to society and circuit discipline. Other Dissenters while deploring Wesleyan authoritarianism, were not averse to trying a similar approach themselves.

The local Sunday School was closely followed, in some cases preceded by, the setting up of a missionary auxiliary—of the Baptist Missionary Society (founded 1792), the London Missionary Society (originally undenominational but increasingly Congregational, founded 1795) and the Methodist Missionary Society (1813). Other smaller denominations, particularly the Methodist sects, were prepared to strain their limited resources to send out missionaries as soon as the home structures had established themselves. Rather late in the field were the New Connexion General Baptists (1818) where physical poverty as well as an ambiguous relationship to the BMS may have been an inhibiting factor, and the Strict Baptists (1862) where theological objections, bred of hyper-Calvinism, had stunted the missionary urge as they had hampered the Sunday School movement earlier on.

Apart from the one feature they shared in common, the imparting to the local churches of a needed sense of wider national—and indeed world—fellowship, the missionary societies reacted on the ecclesiastical bodies they represented in rather different ways. The London Missionary Society, because its 'Fundamental Principle' had been born in an atmosphere of evangelical ecumenicalism which it retained for a few decades longer,[6] gave to Congregationals a feeling of being in the van of enlightened Dissent, of speaking and acting on terms of equality with other Evangelicals, including the Anglicans, of being abreast of the forces of the age, a not unexpected expression of the elitism of Binney and Dale.

The Baptist Missionary Society on the other hand, perhaps because it preceded by so many years and was, as it remains, totally separate from the Baptist Union, had been from the start a supra-denominational missionary agency, coordinating evangelistic effort abroad and at home. Mission for the Baptist was no supplementary activity, but the essential ingredient of his whole vision of what his faith was about, a factor which once more underlines the distinctiveness of this particular tradition. For the Wesleyans it was different again. Here the Missionary Society was founded surprisingly late, a fact due probably to the existence since Wesley's day of a separate and evangelistically-minded Methodism in North America, and to the personal concentration of Wesleyan missionary effort subsequently around the attractive and popular but rather wayward Dr Coke.[7] The MMS was part of the denominational

---

[6] I. M. Fletcher, 'The Fundamental Principle of the London Missionary Society' in *CHST* xix (3–5) (1962–3).

[7] J. Vickers, *Thomas Coke, An Apostle of Methodism* (1969), *passim*.

strategy of the late 1810s and 20s, a further extension of the Wesleyan bureaucracy imposed on the holy community at the behest of the three leaders, Bunting, Watson and Adam Clarke. The strategy was not really directed towards diverting the poor's attention away from 'an otherwise inevitable absorption with their own wretchedness', as Professor Semmel suggests.[8] Rather it was intended to give Wesleyanism a new evangelistic vision after recent numerical setbacks, to direct the eyes of the faithful to scenes of spiritual destitution worse than any at home, and to bind their abiding philanthropic concern within tight denominational channels, while at the same time renewing useful contacts with Exeter Hall in the anti-slavery campaign and kindred colonial concerns. Local Wesleyan congregations, who appear in the records as the most disciplined, bemused and malleable of Dissenters whatever their social rank, were naturally unaware of these machinations on high, and responded with anticipated ardour to missionary promptings.

Reports from the mission field and especially missionary deputations enraptured the home churches. Every society had its heroes and martyrs, the LMS more than most, James Chalmers in the South Seas, James Gilmour in Mongolia, Moffat and Livingstone in Africa. The missionaries, however, saw their task rather differently depending on their background and on the motives of the 'sending' body. Thus Congregationals were keen to vindicate the Independent polity even in the most unlikely contexts such as the tribal society of the South Sea Islands where religious democracy occupied a rather anomalous position within existing structures.[9] The Baptists, such as William Knibb in the West Indies, often to the marked disapproval of the BMS authorities at home, bore heroic evangelical witness against social and political injustice and aided powerfully the movement for emancipation (just as their native converts were to aid in the revolt of 1865 against Governor Eyre).[10] The Wesleyans, true to their societary leanings, simply transplanted their native ethos overseas: they were from the start borne along by a heady vision of vast spiritual conquests, imperial grandeur and the mother country's civilising role. But in general till about mid-century the home churches' motive behind missionary support and missionary giving was a more or less lurid picture of 'multitudes of heathen perishing everlastingly'.

By 1850 the missionary image had changed in certain subtle ways.[11] Difficulties of individual missionaries with their Societies, of both with powerful business interests and especially with the Foreign Office, had

---

[8] B. Semmel, *The Methodist Revolution* (1974), 177. This is one of the very few instances where Semmel seems to subscribe to the New Left's reinterpretation of Methodist history.

[9] J. Montgomery ed., *Journal of the Voyages and Travels of Daniel Tyerman and George Bennet*, I (1831), 292–3.

[10] G. A. Catherall, *William Knibb, Freedom Fighter* (1972); P. Wright, *Knibb, the Notorious* (1973).

[11] An excellent account of the changing missionary image within the Presbyterian Church of England is given by G. A. Hood in *JPHS* xiii (3) (1966).

forced the churches to grapple more seriously with the secular context in which their missionary endeavours were set. Harsh facts like the opium traffic were recognized both for the abuses they were, and yet as the opportunities which had permitted ingress to forbidden lands in the first place. There was in consequence a curious blending of secular opportunism with guilty conscience on the part of the churches, a feeling of unease partly stifled by a crusading spirit of altruism, a vision of the union of the world's 'mightiest empire' with its 'most multitudinous peoples' in a common spiritual quest.

As the years passed these disparate elements distorted the missionary image still further. The missionary appeal to save heathen souls from eternal torment slowly faded, like the idea of Hell itself, into the background, or was confined to the more traditionalist fringe societies like Hudson Taylor's China Inland Mission.[12] The missionary too is no longer cast in the role of self-sacrificing pioneer and prospective martyr: Henry Drummond, Moody's most distinguished academic convert, had done his work well among the University students who were now becoming missionaries in larger numbers than ever before and helping to redefine the missionary's role in terms of a career, with various specialist functions, teaching, medical, pastoral. The sense of the white man's guilt has deepened too, and yet the cultural hubris of late Victorian Imperialism is more pronounced as well, even in the writings of such advanced missionary advocates as Dr Clifford. An incident such as the Boxer Rising could give rise to both opposing sentiments, perplexing and silencing the more conservative missionary enthusiasts. Above all the fact that increasingly the missionary had become captivated by the mission field itself, and had become humbly appreciative and apologetic before the physical beauties and rich cultural traditions of the lands to which he had been sent, had its own effect on the home churches. As early as the 1860s the Presbyterian Mrs Oliphant had lamented the way in which reports from the mission field had become at worst travellers' tales, at best useful illustrative material for the spread of more accurate geographical knowledge.[13] As in the following decades the thirst for entertainment grew, the missionary and his task lent themselves ever more naturally to this popular didactic purpose. The magic lantern completed the process: the Nonconformist missionary entered more intimately into the lives of his admirers at home, but somehow his vocation had been shorn of its pristine glory.

Temperance societies

The chapel temperance society appeared on the scene several decades later than the missionary auxiliary. Chapel men had never been renowned

---

[12] Taylor's theology may have been tradionalist: his adoption of a Chinese lifestyle was considered eccentric and revolutionary.
[13] I. Sellers, 'Mrs M. O. W. Oliphant' in *JPHS* xiv (4) (1971).

for their heavy drinking, but opposition to beer, as distinct from spirits, was a phenomenon of the late 30s and early 40s. Till then even the Sunday School children on their outings had in some cases been regaled with mild ale.[14] The teetotal movement of the 30s associated with sturdy proletarians such as Dunlop and Livesey, was an independent movement of self-respecting artisans, hostile to churches and chapels alike, though inclined to express their arguments in quasi-theological terms, and exhort their audiences with evangelistic fervour. Amateur theologians, they selected scripture texts to suit their purposes and were suspected rightly of being inclined to a disturbing biblical criticism of an old-fashioned deistic kind, and of a sort of ecumenical waywardness which welcomed the cooperation of Unitarians and Roman Catholics. Within a few years, however, Dissent had appreciated the recruitment potential of 'Gospel Temperance', akin in so many ways to religious revivalism, and had begun to absorb it into the chapels, making it respectable, élitist almost, in the process. All the major Nonconformist denominations with the exception of the Wesleyans reacted to the movement in much the same way, and at the same time, though it is curious how the members of smaller sects, particularly Quakers, United Presbyterians and Brethren, were more prominent than most.[15]

By the early 50s, however, Nonconformists were less sure that moral suasion was the panacea for this particular social evil and turned as a reinforcement to schemes of social engineering which became focussed on the drastic legislative solution of total prohibition. The United Kingdom Alliance of 1853 was at first almost wholly Nonconformist in composition, a knot of philanthropic idealistic manufacturers, notably N. Card, C. Jupe, J. Lingford and T. Emmott, taking the lead. Unfortunately this transition to political militancy, as usually happened with Nonconformity, only served to underline the gaucheness and political inexperience of provincial Dissent. What temperance enthusiasm it managed to generate in Westminster was effectively neutralized by the machinations of Gladstone and the indifference of the more politically astute Nonconformist politicians. In any case by the 1870s the Anglican Church was recovering its confidence in its own powers of social control and was infiltrating the national temperance organizations with marked effect. Fortunately for provincial Dissent, however, the tradition of moral suasion never died out even when legislative solutions were being pursued most eagerly. The denominations added temperance committees to their developing bureaucracies in the Victorian years precisely so that they could encourage the formation of adult organizations and Bands of Hope for the children of the local church. Popular temperance was still a viable proposition and received

---

[14] J. B. Goodman ed., *Memoirs of a Victorian Cabinet Maker, James Hopkinson* (1968), 70–71.
[15] B. Harrison, *Drink and The Victorians* (1971), 164.

a belated boost when the Garibaldian Lifeboat Crews appeared on the scene in the 1860s. It is hardly surprising therefore that the Moody-Sankey revival gave a renewed impetus to moral suasion. Moody's friend William Noble introduced the Blue Ribbon movement into England, and by 1882 bodies such as the Good Templars could regard 'religious' and 'temperance' conversion as the obverse and reverse of the same spiritual coin. Once again we notice how double-edged the revivalism of the last quarter of the century appears to be: on the one hand men were, as Brian Harrison has shown,[16] being drawn out of the world rather than being seen as the leaven which would transform it into the Kingdom. On the other hand the missionary urge led to an intense activism, particularly in the towns, where Dissenters launched a variety of counter-attractive organizations, Coffee Palaces, British Workman Public Houses, Cocoa Rooms and People's Cafes, and, inspired by Chamberlain and Cadbury who had both broken with the United Kingdom Alliance, turned increasingly to municipal solutions, in particular to municipal control of licensing and opening laws. Local option was now the Nonconformist rallying cry.

What was the long-term significance of this absorption of temperance enthusiasm into the life and witness of the Dissenting churches? For some historians, especially Dr Harrison, it is another instance of the secularizing process. It channelled religious energies into party politics: it substituted a moral reform crusade for traditional (and increasingly embarrassing), divisive and outworn contentions over problems liturgical and doctrinal: it provided, especially in its outspoken contempt for inspirational and textual controversies, a welcome relief from the gradual disappearance of the age-old certainties. Yet a careful reading of the temperance literature of the time (or of the temperance sections of Dissenting hymnals) suggests that it could well have had an opposite effect, driving the churches especially in later years back to that very pietistic heritage which their national leaders were confident that they had gladly left behind as soon as emancipation had dawned.

Again, was the temperance movement a solvent of the individualism of Protestant Dissent? The community life of the chapels was, as Beatrice Webb observed in Bacup, a kind of religious socialism: so perhaps in advocating legislative solutions Dissent was stressing this latent collectivism which underlay the individualism with which their social witness was normally clothed. Perhaps, too, the sheer enormity of the problem and the complexity of the vested interests which supported it imparted to the 'outsider' mentality of its Dissenting assailants a radical quality of which they had not hitherto imagined they were possessed.

Certainly Dissenters, high and low, searched their souls over the most acceptable solution to what they generally referred to as 'England's curse, England's shame'. How could they, laissez-fairist in their basic outlook, justify themselves at the Last Day if they opposed penal

[16] *Ibid*, 194.

taxation of the Drink Interest or municipal control and if their opposition to such a significant extension of collectivism led to a perpetuation of the very evil they wished to destroy? It was all very worrying to confirmed individualists: little wonder that T. H. Green's hard thought-out solutions to the dilemma over drink regulation had a peculiar attraction for Nonconformists.

On a more humdrum level their temperance witness may have had other effects, psychological and social, on the local churches. There is much evidence to suggest, for example, that temperance could be a grand emotional purgative enabling men who had suffered from centuries of second class citizenship to vent their suppressed rage, by concentrating it on one particular abuse, against the whole establishment in church and state, and the entire life-style of the traditional ruling class which had harried them ever since 1662: in which case of course a very real social evil could easily become a symbol of a clash between rival cultures—a point not lost on Gladstone when he came to draw the teeth of militant Dissent.

Within the chapel community on the other hand, the temperance organization might become, like the Sunday School, a weapon against the ministry or against a commanding social group. It might promote contact with other chapels of the same or different denominations: it might, depending on circumstances, isolate the chapel still further from the community around, especially in a small village where it rivalled the public house as the focus of social intercourse. It might be a source of recruitment of new members, like the Sunday School, or it might be successfully adapted later on in the century to cater for the developing leisure ethic of the time.

It might again be a symbol of the late Victorian embourgeoisement of the Chapel communities which even in mid-century still contained a good cross-section of social classes within their ranks. In this case the chapel temperance society may be seen, by the century's end, as the bastion of those who believed in self-help and self-improvement—and had achieved their ambitions. Temperance which, like Sabbatarianism, had started off as a popular movement, became in proletarian eyes increasingly a symbol of upper-class dominance as the century progressed.[17] Whatever forms of state intervention the Victorian working-class may have welcomed (and they were not many) interference with their drinking habits or their Sunday sporting pursuits on the part of a backward-looking Nonconformity was certainly not among them. In the rambling, disjointed diatribes of the Tory-radical J. R. Stephens against the temperance movement of the 30s we may read in anticipation the outrage felt by the humbler classes against this meddlesome interference later on in the century, as well as the sort of arguments they would regularly employ in their own defence. (In their attitudes to the

[17] B. Harrison, 'Religion and Recreation in Nineteenth Century England' in *Past and Present*, No. 38 (1967).

recreational habits of the Victorian working-class the Dissenters just could not do right. Thus the Unitarians, followed at some distance by the Congregationals, who took a very progressive attitude to the Sabbath, supported the National Sunday League and secured the Sunday opening of parks, promoted public concerts, and earned general approval. This however they forfeited by taking the lead in forming local branches of the RSPCA, whose interference with popular sports involving animals led to particularly strong working-class disapproval.)

There is an additional complicating factor in the complexities of the nineteenth-century temperance movement, the ambiguous position once again occupied by the Wesleyan body. Here the divisiveness and theological waywardness of the early teetotal campaign were looked upon with particular disfavour. Moderate drinking in the 1840s was at Conference instigation taken as a kind of badge of Wesleyan membership, and rigorously enforced on students in the theological institution. (This occassioned yet another schism when in Cornwall the Teetotal Wesleyan Methodists hived off from the parent body.[18]) But in the 1860s the hierarchy was faced with a growing temperance movement in the local churches, yielded to such pressure, and gave its official imprimatur to Gospel Temperance activities (not of course to the UK Alliance, with which Wesleyan relations were always strained).

But Wesleyan suspicions died hard. In 1883 W. B. Pope, preaching on Romans 15, identified in a sophisticated and thoroughly biblical manner the 'strong' as those with a sound, balanced attitude to life, and the 'weak' as the ethical faddists. (The implied reference to temperance fanatics was obvious: most Nonconformists would have argued in exactly the opposite way, and seen the weak as the drink-sodden); even as late as the 90s the Wesleyans were still demanding as a matter of connexional discipline that all Wesleyan temperance societies contain both total abstainers and moderationists. Politically they had advanced no further than local option, and even this was abandoned hastily in the first decade of the new century when a spate of evangelistic pledge-signing crusades of the old Gospel Temperance sort were officially sponsored. (The Wesleyans were perhaps fortunate in this self-imposed isolation, for it enabled them to be among the first to recognize in the late 80s the alcoholic as the victim of a psychosomatic disorder, and to open small homes for his reclamation.)

It is finally temperance which, more than any other concern, helps to highlight the differences between the minor Methodist bodies which are such a puzzle to the historians. The Primitive Methodists, for example, had been among the first to adopt temperance principles, yet were among the last to erect denominational machinery to express this enthusiasm, a neat illustration this of the Primitives' peculiar facility for combining evangelistic enterprise with social action, revivalism and

[18] M. S. Edwards, 'The Teetotal Wesleyan Methodists' in *PWHS* xxxiii Pts 3–4 (1961).

radicalism, while remaining psychologically incapable of distinguishing between the two. The Bible Christians as the most a-political and holiness-orientated of all the Methodist bodies eschewed political action of any kind and consistently determined to know no other temperance than the Gospel sort. On the other hand the ultra democrats of the United Methodist Free Churches were particularly keen on implementing a political programme of temperance reform, and gearing their denominational machinery to this end. Only the New Connexion's temperance contribution seems to tally with the developing attitudes of the older Dissent.[19]

One other major institution, generally overlooked by the historians, had in a large number of cases been added to the local Nonconformist church by the mid-nineteenth century, the tract-distribution society. As Methodist class leaders wandered the streets of towns and villages visiting the members entrusted to their care, so Baptist and Congregational deacons took increasingly to the habit of exercising a similar pastoral oversight of a selected area within the vicinity of their church. A 'Local', 'Look-out', 'Visiting' or 'Missionary' Committee was often formed to coordinate these efforts. Tract distribution likewise seems originally to have been an evangelistic technique born of the Methodist revival, and borrowed at a fairly early date by the Old Dissent.[20] Lay leaders in all branches of Nonconformity pursued their calling in the disposal of vast quantities of tracts, either gratis or preferably by loaning them, for a return visit provided an opportunity for exhortation and the securing of converts or the strengthening of chapel links. Tract distribution was especially resorted to in time of spiritual dearth when the revival impulse had been spent, and after the opening of a new church in a recently developed area. Sometimes the impulse would arise spontaneously from the organizing church which would itself print the tracts: at others the resources of a national body, the Religious Tract Society, would be called upon. Visiting, cottage-meetings and tract-distribution were thus both an important lay evangelizing agency and Victorian Dissent's most obvious borrowing of the Methodist practice of pastoral care exercised by the church members themselves. And once again such a powerful illustration of the priesthood of believers in action could hardly fail to reassure Dissenting activists as to the moral superiority of their system to the priestly tyranny of the Roman Church.

The institutional church

Correctly anticipating the future development of Nonconformity from his own Birmingham experience the Reverend J. A. James wrote

[19] G. T. Brake, *Drink Ups and Downs* (1974), 63f.
[20] M. R. Sheard, 'Methodist Tract-Visiting Societies in the early Nineteenth Century' in *PWHS* xxxix, Pt. 2 (1973).

enthusiastically in his *Earnestness In Churches* (1848) of the 'thoroughly working church' where all members should be like 'bees of a hive, all busy', 'each in his own department, and all adding to the common stock'. Fifty years later P. T. Forsyth saw late Victorian departmentalism in churches as the harbinger of secularism, a surrender to the social and cultural pressures of the outside world. In 1907, the very year of R. J. Campbell's outrageous New Theology movement, this Congregational high-churchman pleaded for a Christianity 'which antagonizes culture without denying its place. Culture asks but half a Gospel, and half a Gospel is no Gospel. We must of course go some way to meet the world, but when we do meet we must do more than greet . . . the world which is not unready to profess itself enchanted with Christ must be converted to Him and subdued and made not merely a better world but a world reconciled and redeemed.'[21] Did the Institutional Church of late nineteenth century Dissent merit either James's encomium or Forsyth's magisterial rebuke?

The institutional church developed at first by accident, later by design. As early as the 1830s and 40s Unitarians, inspired by influences as various as Dr Tuckerman in America and Dr Chalmers in Glasgow, had founded Domestic Missions in the poorer areas of great cities, but their philanthropic efforts had attracted less sympathy from Orthodox Dissent than the purely evangelistic City Missions which David Nasmith had founded in London, Liverpool and elsewhere. These were a type of supra-denominational evangelistic work which, like the contemporary more specialist missions to seamen, tramping artizans or prisoners, were actively supported by Nonconformists and which while their initial impetus lasted into the 1840s gave the impression that the socially depressed were being cared for and reclaimed.

Around the year 1850, however, Congregationals and Baptists in particular became deeply worried by the spectre of working-class alienation and began to arrange special services of their own for workingmen, on a Saturday afternoon or Sunday evening, the Reverend B. Grant taking the lead among the former, H. S. Brown of Liverpool among the latter. Difficulties over the distance of working-class residential areas from the central chapels, over working-class embarrassment at attending socially superior places of worship, and over the unavailability of seats because of the pew rent system, led in the following two decades to a rash of mission halls established by enterprising laymen or women in working-class districts: Brown's Myrtle Street launched approximately a dozen of these, some in purpose-built chapels, some in converted cottages, a couple in rooms over commercial premises.[22]

Evangelism and church extension were the primary objectives of this home missionary enterprise, whether springing up from within the

---

[21] P. T. Forsyth, *Positive Preaching and The Modern Mind* (1907), 89.
[22] H. S. Brown, *Autobiography and Commonplace Book* (1887), 90f.

local churches or initiated by connexional agency. Disagreement prevails as to the respective merits of these different approaches, and Professor Inglis has argued that the connexional Wesleyan and Congregational Home Missionary organizations which sprang to life in the mid-50s were both starved of funds, concentrated far too much on the countryside rather than the towns, and were wasteful of the efforts and talents expended on them.[23] But such local studies as are available show that these strictures hardly apply to all the schemes pioneered in the towns and cities, many of which were non- or supra-denominational, or went unmentioned in the Churches' Year Books.

Gradually and inevitably social work, of either a philanthropic, 'improving' or culture-dispensing variety impinged on this original pattern of evangelistic activity in response to the secular currents abroad in the second half of the century. The pressures were of several kinds, but four affected Dissent considerably. The first was a heightened awareness of the social problem. The publication of Andrew Mearns's *Bitter Cry of Outcast London* (1883) greatly quickened the Nonconformist appreciation of the social destitution of the urban masses; the guilt-ridden response to this Congregational tract by the Dissenting churches showed that few publications had such a traumatic and lasting effect on the organized religious conscience of the day.[24]

The second pressure was very much the reverse of the first: the increasingly home-orientated direction of the life of the suburbs, and where the high-walled villas led in the cultivation of domestic privacy, the respectable terraced rows of the working-class would not be far behind. This trend is seen especially in the change in quality and size of the denominational magazines in the 1880s and 90s, which now incorporate serialized novels and are full of photographs and drawings, hopelessly inferior in intellectual quality and challenge to their predecessors, but obviously catering for a new thirst for amusement and non-too-demanding edification within the confines of the home.

The third is the rise of organized professional entertainment. Till about 1880 in town and village alike, the public house had been almost the sole competitor with the chapel or church as the focus of the social life of the community. (Hence some of the enthusiasm with which prominent Nonconformists like Henry Richard MP endeavoured to secure the exclusion of public houses from new housing developments in later Victorian cities). Afterwards, however, the capitalist promoters of leisure activities, particularly professional football, provided what was even then an alternative and evidently welcome outlet for the interests and enthusiasms of the working population.[25]

Finally for religious bodies which, in the towns at least, had in the

[23] K. S. Inglis, *op. cit.*, 14.
[24] A. Mearns, *The Bitter Cry of Outcast London* (Leicester University reprint, 1970); A. S. Whol, 'The Bitter Cry of Outcast London' in *International Review of Social History* xiii (1968), 189f.
[25] S. Yeo, *Religious Organizations In Crisis* (1975), 136f.

past competed and competed successfully with the Established Church in offering to a buying public their own brands of Christianity as so many consumer goods, the growth of retail stores parading their rivalries along the High Street increased the sense of competitiveness among the chapels, for they too depended for their continuing existence on what in secular, maybe even religious, terms was basically the gospel of success.

Nonconformists therefore both feared and welcomed the most powerful urban trends of the age. Private activities such as hobbies or the passive spectatorship of sporting displays, both features of the new leisure ethic, conflicted with their most deeply-held beliefs that voluntary commitment to the social agency, organized voluntaryism as the noblest spur to public good and private well-being, was the outward form which their inward religious convictions most naturally assumed. Conversely as society was added to society, Savings Banks to Dorcas Groups, Tontine Societies to Benefit Clubs, Literary Circles to Chapel Mock-Parliaments, Christian Endeavours to Boys and Girls Brigades, the Football Club to the Adult School, the Brotherhood to the PSA, as organizations spawned yet more organizations, forming what Charles Booth called the 'penumbra' of chapel agencies, Nonconformists could feel proud that their foresight and enthusiasm had provided the resources in leadership and buildings which in many localities were the envy of Churchmen and secularists alike.

Primarily of course their efforts were directed to preserving the solidarity and unity of the chapel community itself. If bazaars, magic lanterns and the ubiquitous tea urn now characterized weeknight activities in the chapel, they justified themselves in that the crowds flocked in. But this idea of religion as entertainment was bound to rub off onto the Sabbath acts of worship themselves. When with the aid of choirs and choral items, solos and organ voluntaries, affected prayers and 'topical' preaching the religious service has itself become a form of entertainment, we need not be surprised, as Dr Currie reminds us[26] when the very terms in which the congregation expressed its approval of what it received on Sunday, 'a good time', or a 'blessing', point to the same subtle metamorphosis. (Such language is tepid and maudlin when compared with the old, unbowdlerized Puritan expressions still used in some circles at the start of the century, when for example his hearers denounced a doctrinally empty and experimentally barren preacher with the words, 'thou art a dry breast'.)

Moreover if (as C. F. G. Masterman pointed out at the time and G. H. McLeod has demonstrated from his examination of the life of the London churches in the three decades before 1914[27]) active ministers could build up their own flocks by means of institutionalizing their church structures, it would only be at the expense of neighbouring, less successful churches whose area of support would contract in proportion

[26] R. Currie, *op. cit.*, 138.
[27] H. McLeod, *Class and Religion In The Late Victorian City* (1974).

to their success. Entrepreneurial rivalry can not simply be seen as a clash between church and chapel: it affected other Dissenting denominations, even weaker churches of the same body. The phenomenal success of ministers such as Clifford at Westbourne Park or Charles Leach at Queen's Park Congregational should be seen in this light.

Secondly Nonconformists were drawn to the Institutional Church as a means of securing cultural domination over the neighbourhood. As the chapel deacons, before appointing a new minister, enquired anxiously how successful the candidates had been in their previous pastorates in raising up and maintaining flourishing institutions, they obviously had in mind a church building to which all age groups, all classes and all interests could gravitate and where all could indulge in something attractive enough to occupy their leisure hours. This again may serve to remind us that the cultural aggression associated with H. P. Hughes and the more assertive interpreters of the Nonconformist conscience at the national level has its roots planted firmly in the outlook of the local churches.

In all this however there were appalling dangers. It was as if the Institutional Church was leading purblind chapel activists into a variety of traps from which they have ever since been struggling to get free. First there was the bricks and mortar trap. So greatly had the 'ecclesiastical plant' of the typical institutional church expanded that problems of financing and maintaining the same were already becoming acute by 1900 and were threatening to sap the energies of the mother church.

Again, the institutional church was trapped by formidable pressures both from above and below. From above, as the number of generous local donors dried up with the passing of Sir Titus Salt's generation of altruistic Nonconformist philanthropists and their successors either fell away, conformed or turned to their own leisure pursuits—sailing, shooting and the like—the chapels were compelled to rely all the more on central connexional funds or else on mortgages with building societies (even in some cases on the issue of debenture stocks to finance new projects). This 'nationalizing' tendency which threatened to curb drastically the independence of the local church was reinforced by the fact that so many of the new Institutions, particularly the uniformed ones and the Christian Endeavour, were also nationally-orientated bodies, their supporters owing a primary loyalty to the organization, and allegiance to the chapel only in so far as their branch happened to meet on a particular set of premises.

From below there arose an insistent demand from the various cultural and consuming sub-groups which clustered round the chapel that special arrangements, even special forms of worship, should be provided for themselves alone, thus shattering the church idea into fragments, transforming the mission halls and subagencies from being feeders to the mother church into ends in themselves, even encouraging the chapel planners, in the words of Dr Yeo, to devise services and entertainment 'not in relation to the felt needs of members but in relation to the supposed needs of potential customers'.[28]

Thirdly, a vast influx of uncommitted persons into the life of the local church raised in an acute form the question which had always haunted Victorian Dissent, the relationship between members and adherents, the whole thorny problem of 'joining', 'belonging to' or simply 'going to' a particular church. As the assumption of church membership, save among the Wesleyans and conservative (as opposed to open-membership) Baptists, was now a relatively undemanding process, the chapels could be expected to recruit heavily from the sub-agencies attached to them. Even so the numbers of casual adherents were increasing out of all proportion to those of actual members, and Mudie Smith's survey of London Congregational churches which was contributed to the *Daily News* in 1902 and 1903 showed that adherents even in the regular worshipping congregations were by that time outnumbering members, by approximately seven to five.

Finally there may be what Dr Kent has identified as the subculture trap.[29] For all the intense and disastrous self-exaltation of Nonconformity's clerical leadership over the supposed triumph of the Non-conformist conscience after 1889, and for all the Anglicans' reassertion of *their* religious primacy from the 1870s onwards, both bodies were in their dedication to outworn ideals and forms of social control becoming part of the religious subculture of the times. Ignored as an irritant by the bulk of town dwellers who demanded from the churches only the *rites de passage* and an occasional 'good time' at Harvest Festivals or the Whit Walks, even their sabbatarian time structures, as the weekend and July holiday habits spread, were highlighted as the antiquated survivals of upper-class cultural leadership which they undoubtedly were. Kent thus questions the thesis expounded by R. W. Dale and his contemporaries that somehow Nonconformity came to terms with and offered a distinctive approach to the Victorian town in a manner which the negative and backward-looking Establishment never even attempted to emulate. But do the complex achievements of the Institutional church, whatever their internal contradictions, really lend themselves to this depressing conclusion? Only when the delicate balance between the sub-agencies viewed as tools of social aggression or as opportunities for popular self-expression has been successfully struck by a painstaking examination of the Institutional church in action in a wide range of different localities can this question be properly resolved.[30]

[28] S. Yeo, 'A Contextual View of Religious Organization' in M. Hill, ed., *A Sociological Year Book of Religion in Britain*, vi (1973), 228.

[29] J. H. S. Kent, 'The Role of Religion', *loc. cit.*, 159.

[30] Dr Kent cites the example of the Reverend F. B. Meyer (Baptist) as providing a particularly ludicrous example of Nonconformist culture-dispensing to working-class women. But Meyer was a consummate actor, especially in the company of doting female admirers. No one would have relished more than he the delightful absurdity of a background of singing canaries for his weeknight lectures.

4 People and Churches

The geography of Dissent

Nineteenth-century Dissent as a geographical phenomenon may be studied from both a regional (macro-) and a more localized, village/town (micro-) perspective. Regionally an interesting pattern emerges. The Old Dissenters, Unitarians, Congregationals and Baptists, strengthen their hold on areas of traditional strength, while expanding more slowly into regions where previously they had been under-represented or non-existent. Thus the Unitarians were concentrated heavily in the West Midlands, Lancashire, Cheshire and the West Riding, the West Country, London and the Southeast. In the cities they were weak numerically but socially significant out of all proportion to their membership rolls.

The Congregationals were strongest in the eastern parts of Wessex, in London itself, in the East Midlands and East Anglia and fairly powerful in Lancashire and Yorkshire. The Particular Baptists flourished in the old Puritan areas of the East Midlands, particularly Northamptonshire, in Wiltshire and the West, and were slightly less strong than the Congregationals in the Industrial North. New Connexion General Baptists however added to Baptist strength in Lincolnshire, Derbyshire, Leicestershire, Nottinghamshire (particularly in the lace and hosiery areas), with significant extensions into the cotton and woollen towns of Lancashire and the West Riding. Orthodox Presbyterianism was heavily concentrated in the extreme north, though isolated pockets were to be found in areas of Scottish emigration in different parts of England, particularly sea-port towns. As the century progressed, more and more chapels were built in the towns and fewer in the countryside. There was also a marked shift in denominational strengths to the Southeast. Here the churches were clearly following in the wake of powerful demographic trends.[1]

The situation of the Methodists was rather different. Robert Currie in relation to the country as a whole, B. Greaves for Yorkshire and M. Cook for Devon have noted how in areas where the Church of England was weak, in the out-townships of large parishes, in industrial villages,

[1] J. D. Gay, *The Geography of Religion in England* (1971), 156ff.

in large parishes with non-resident clergymen, Wesleyanism took an immediate hold.[2] This contrasts strongly with the Old Dissent which had taken root and in many cases continued to flourish in regions of Anglican strength. But in areas of virtual Anglican eclipse, such as London, Warwickshire, Southeast Lancashire and parts of Kent, even Methodism failed to prosper. In such places anti-Anglican sentiment based on hostility to tithes seems to have produced a mentality hostile to religion altogether.

Wesleyanism thus built up its fastnesses in the East, the Midlands and the Northeast, the West Riding and Lincolnshire, Cornwall and Dorset. Wesleyan frontal growth was checked, as we have seen, by 1819, and tailed off perceptibly in the latter half of the century. Memberships still grew but not in proportion to population growth, while there is a general shift to the Southeast, London and the Home Counties comparable to that in other denominations, together with less significant shifts into the West Midlands and Lancashire.

The development of the Methodist sects is to be understood in the light of this pattern of Wesleyan strengths and weaknesses. The older-established bodies undoubtedly filled up many gaps in areas neglected by the original Connexion. Thus the New Connexion established a line of churches in the West Midland counties and another east of the Pennines from Nottinghamshire to the Scottish border. The Primitive Methodists too thrust their powerful evangelistic arms into geographical and socially depressed areas relatively untouched by the Wesleyan itinerants—from Staffordshire westwards through the 'Cheshire Round' into Shropshire and South Lancashire, southward via the vast Brinkworth Round into Wiltshire, Oxfordshire and Bedfordshire, northwards into Hull, an evangelistic centre comparable to Burslem itself and thence into the East Riding, Durham and the Northeast, and eastwards into Nottinghamshire, Cambridgeshire, Lincolnshire and Norfolk. Even the Bible Christians filled in the gaps in Wesleyan activity in Cornwall, and particularly in Devon.

With the rise of the Wesleyan Methodist Association in the later 30s however, a different pattern emerges. The Associationists recruit largely from established Wesleyan societies, flourish in areas of Wesleyan strength, which is consequently diminished, and thus display from the start 'lateral' rather than 'frontal' growth, and continue to do so, save for a few years in the 1860s, right to the end of the period. The same seems to be true also of the Wesleyan Reformers of 1849. Growth rates in all the minor Methodist bodies fall off after mid-century, and quite sharply after 1880, and it is then that lateral growth patterns are transformed subtly from expansion at the expense of others into expansion by joint endeavours with them, and the ecumenical idea is really born. In some areas indeed where individual

[2] R. Currie, 'A Micro-Theory of Methodist Growth' in *PWHS* xxxvi Pt. 3 (1967).

congregations were hopelessly isolated and cut off from the fellowship of kindred churches, the struggle was abandoned at a very early date, and union with a more powerfully established denomination was sought. Such happened to several Methodist New Connexion causes in Cornwall, and to the tiny handful of General Baptist New Connexion churches in the Southeast.[3]

It should also be noted that peculiarities in the local economy, its class structure and family patterns will naturally modify these neatly constructed models in minor details. Thus D. G. Hey from his examinations of Nonconformity in South Yorkshire is rather wary of Dr Currie's conclusions, finding that the Old Dissent tended to be strongest where the Church of England was weakest. Likewise Methodism was here as successful in Old Dissenting areas as in those previously untouched by Dissent. Again local circumstances rendered the Baptists particularly weak, and the Methodist New Connexion more radical and proletarian than elsewhere.[4]

Broad regional variations and patterns of growth have attracted less attention from the historians than an evaluation of the conditions prevailing in different types of urban and rural settlement as fillips to or dissuasives from the practice of Dissent. From his examination of the growth of Puritanism in the countryside Professor Everitt has gone on to explore the later effects of the Evangelical Awakening and subsequent revivals on the whole pattern of nineteenth-century rural Nonconformity.[5] His conclusions, based on the evidence of four different shires, are probably applicable to most others. Just as the disintegrated property patterns of the decayed market towns enabled their inhabitants to 'snap their fingers' at the Establishment and embrace Dissent, so areas of scattered and woodland settlements, especially in Devon, Northants, Shropshire, East Anglia and the West Riding, favoured a similar development. In open and 'divided' villages, villages with absentee landlords, with several subsidiary townships or with large groups of independent craftsmen, social control was difficult to enforce or missing altogether, and Dissent flourished, notably in 'dark corners' and in parish boundary settlements. Only in the closed, nucleated villages was the Establishment in effective control, and Dissent banished. Even here however the Methodist revolution was to make a profound difference.

Methodism, perhaps because it often arose under the aegis of the parish church, became successful in gentry-dominated areas (which means particularly close-knit and 'arable' villages) where the Old Dissent was largely missing. It also in both its Wesleyan and Primitive

[3] M. S. Edwards, 'The New Connexion at Breage' in *Journal of the Cornish Methodist Historical Association* i (7) (May 1963); F. Buffard, *The Kent and Sussex Baptist Associations* (1963), 63f.
[4] D. G. Hey, 'The Pattern of Nonconformity in South Yorkshire' in *Northern History* viii (1973).
[5] A. Everitt, *The Pattern of Rural Dissent; The Nineteenth Century* (1972).

varieties flourished in the new canal- and railway-dominated communities. The villagers of early nineteenth-century England, it is clear, experienced population growth, rapid mobility and a sense of rootlessness and alienation just as much as the new populations of the towns and their need for the warm fellowship of the chapel was equally pressing.

So considerable was Wesleyanism's rural achievement that it became a conviction of Bunting's that his Connexion was and must remain the religion of the English countryside. If therefore much Wesleyan like much Congregational Home Missionary activity was from the mid-century onwards devoted to the villages at the expense of the towns there was sound historical reason for this particular deployment of denominational resources.

Yet it was just at this time that Nonconformists began to lament the disappearance of the yeoman and the tenant farmer and the crippling effects of rural emigration on the life of the churches. The cry is heard from the Strict and Particular Baptists, whose Wessex strongholds were in the next seventy years to perish almost completely, as early as the 1860s.[6] By the 1870s the Baptist Union was advising the government to sponsor a 'class of small-holding proprietors' to shore up their country churches, the Congregationals were launching a new Church Aid and Home Missionary Society (1878), and the Primitives, who were still largely a rural body, were beginning to decry the long, slow drift of agricultural labourers to the colonies or the towns. Of all the denominations the Primitives had the most to lose by the late Victorian crisis in the countryside.

Mrs Poyser's remark in *Adam Bede* that only townsfolk turn to Methodism, and that no farmers were bitten by 'them maggots' was obviously contradicted by the facts: Methodism was well-established in towns and villages alike at the opening of the century. The growth of urban Nonconformity is, however, only just beginning to be studied in depth. One factor which is already emerging is that the division between town and countryside, beloved of historians in the past, is till the last decades of the century, a misleading one. Labour migration, which is now recognized for the short-distance process it undoubtedly was, meant that if Nonconformity was already strong in a particular area, urban development which occurs therein will copy in its religious aspect the character of the surrounding countryside, thus explaining for example why Primitive Methodism was so strong in the cathedral city of Chester.

Furthermore, life- and work-patterns in the new towns were still remarkably localized: the communal atmosphere of village life was thus easily transplanted into the towns and the degree of cultural shock experienced when the transition was made has been seriously

---

[6] R. Oliver, *The Strict Baptist Chapels of England*, V, Wiltshire and The West (1968), 7f.

exaggerated. Even where long-distance migration takes place, such as that of Cornish tin-miners to the new haematite iron fields of the Northwest in the later nineteenth century, forms of religious adherence are quickly transplanted—hence the numbers of Bible Christian churches in the Furness district. Again, even where both of these phenomena (short-distance migration and the new view of the Victorian town as an agglomerate of small, socially homogeneous units) are not present or are being eroded by the coming of cheap transport facilities between the workingman's place of abode and his work (a late development in any case), working-class life continues doggedly to correspond to a rural rather than to a supposed urban stereotype.

London itself, the least localized and most heterogeneous of Victorian cities, provides the best example of these persisting tendencies.[7] Thus the northeast suburbs are heavily Nonconformist, drawing on the character of neighbouring Essex, but the southwest has a much feebler record of Nonconformist activity, no doubt reflecting the weakness of Surrey Dissent. Even whole regions partake of this character: how else are the high Nonconformist attendances in the 1851 census in the East Midlands to be explained alongside their poor performance in the West Midlands, save on this town-country analogue? Many of the surprising urban variations in the same census may in fact be elucidated if only the structures of the neighbouring villages are taken into account, particularly Nonconformist strength in areas such as West Cornwall, the Northants boot-making district, Northeast Lancashire and parts of the Black Country and the Potteries.

Even so, the larger the towns became, the smaller the correspondence to the adjacent countryside, and by the 1850s Nonconformists of all kinds had begun to worry about the problem of suburbanization, by which they meant the retreat of their more affluent supporters away from the city centres to more distant residential areas. Wesleyans and Congregationals, representing the higher income groups among Dissenters, were naturally the most concerned, and their chapel building programmes of the 60s were particularly impressive.

For the former connexional and circuit machinery worked with almost military precision: new positions were occupied across the map, and the polished woodwork of their large new chapels suggested for this exciting decade a name long remembered in Wesleyan circles— the 'mahogany age'. Congregational expansion into suburbia was a more random affair.[8] The enthusiasm generated by the 1862 bicentenary celebrations counted for much, as did the county and district unions (though these could vary enormously in effectiveness), as did the benefactions of a galaxy of wealthy Congregational businessmen, as did the individual initiative of a single, self-appointed regional

[7] H. McLeod, *op. cit.*, 70f.
[8] R. Tudor Jones, *op. cit.*, 295f.

boss, Joshua Wilson in mid-Victorian London, and later E. T. Egg in metropolitan Essex.[9]

The presence on the edge of expanding towns of village chapels which could be absorbed or enlarged also counted for much, and these in both denominations were fortunately fairly numerous. But meanwhile the lot of the inner-belt churches became more and more parlous, especially for Congregationals who lacked the advantages of a circuit system in which the powerful felt constrained to support the weak. Sometimes their down-town causes were allowed to sink, sometimes a determined effort was made to prop them up with subventions, but as time passed difficulties mounted, and the Congregationals in 1895 appointed a special Church Extension Committee, an oddly named body, for its primary task was to deal with the dire needs of the crumbling chapels of central London.

Artisan housing development was another problem for the churches. From their elitist strongholds in the suburbs Congregationals built 'working class' churches and then complained when their artisan congregations failed to make them self-supporting. The Congregationals became the first of the main Dissenting denominations to begin to fail conspicuously in the towns of late Victorian England. The natural advantage which the Census of 1851 showed them enjoying in Sheffield, London, Bristol, Coventry and Southampton they quickly lost, particularly to the Methodists and Baptists.

Wesleyans planted their large 'missionary' chapels like Martello towers in suburbs such as London's Camberwell, Liverpool's Kirkdale or Birmingham's Handsworth and extended their spiritual, educational and eleemosynary disciplines with considerable success. But it was here, and in the older, more depressed inner areas that the Baptists, who occupy a position between the middle and artisan classes (Particulars inclining to the former, Generals to the latter), and the Methodist sects (low-status Nonconformity, as it is sometimes called) made their most effective challenge. All these bodies, like the Salvation Army later on, were prone to violent fluctuations in fortune, but all built cheaply, and rarely put up a building to accommodate more than about four hundred. In some working-class districts this type of Dissent fared particularly well, as in towns such as Barnsley and Pontefract in South Yorkshire, and Hanley and Longton in the Potteries, though here single-occupation communities seem to have been far more amenable to penetration, especially by the Primitives, than towns of diversified employment, and this factor may help to explain why in certain working class wards Nonconformity of any type was virtually unrepresented, and why in others it was predominant.

These urban successes meant that when the Nonconformist denominations saught to reinforce their triumph of 1851 by publishing

[9] J. H. Taylor, 'London Congregational Churches Since 1850', in *CHST* xx (1) (1965).

more statistics in 1872 and again a decade later[10] they showed, on the one hand, that they were still adding to their accommodation far more rapidly than the Anglicans, and were still increasing their attendances in absolute terms. But by this time faction fights were beginning to break out as to which kinds of theology (whether of the hot and red or of the liberal/social gospel type) were best calculated to ensure success. The more sociologically-minded Nonconformists observed that large towns of slow growth as well as smaller towns were still their happiest environment, and that their relative failure with the working class as a whole was relieved by their success with occupational groups such as the miners of Durham or the fishermen of the East Anglian ports. But perhaps the saddest conclusion to be drawn was the decline in Nonconformist progress relative to population growth, a decline reinforced by the failure at both ends of the geographical spectrum—in cities of most rapid population growth and in the villages and hamlets where their traditional strength had always lain.[11]

Dissenters and social evolution

How at different times did the individual Dissenter regard himself and the world in which he lived? In a century as fraught with change and challenge as the nineteenth it would have been surprising if ideas and presuppositions were to remain constant throughout. Indeed the Dissenters of the 1800s and the 1890s inhabited widely divergent cultural milieux, and their outlooks differed accordingly.

Superficially it would be enough to describe our late Georgian Nonconformist in the manner of Dr Dale, as one addicted to a rhetorical in contrast to his forebear's systematic theology, as displaying a preference for existential rather than intellectual preaching (and thinking). In truth there is more to his basic mental attitudes than this. We might for example note his interest in history and anxiety to justify his choice of Dissent by citing precedent: Bradburn, Pawson and Joseph Sutcliffe among the Wesleyans are here matched by Walter Wilson, David Bogue and James Bennett among the Congregationals, and by Joseph Ivimey, Robert Hall and William Steadman among the Baptists.[12]

Historical insights, however, combined with the impact of contemporary events to produce a variety of differing assumptions among

[10] These have been examined for Liverpool by R. B. Walker in *J Ecc H* xix (1968) and by I. Sellers, Liverpool Nonconformity (unpublished Keele PhD thesis, 1969), 46f.

[11] R. Currie, *Methodism Divided*, 85ff.

[12] S. Bradburn, *Methodism Set Forth and Defended* (1792); J. Pawson, *A Chronological Catalogue . . . of the Travelling Preachers* (1795); J. Sutcliffe, *A Review of Methodism* (1805); W. Wilson, *History and Antiquities of Dissenting Churches In London* (4 vols, 1808–14); D. Bogue and J. Bennett, *History of Dissenters* (4 vols, 180–12); J. Ivimey, *A History of The English Baptists* (4 vols, 1811–30); R. Hall, *Sermons, Essays and Reviews* (1838); T. Steadman, *Memoir of W. Steadman* (1838).

this generation of Dissenters. Some, still a large number, were satisfied by the defensive arguments which sprang from a century's experience of grudging toleration. Bogue and Bennett, for example in the section entitled Particular Reasons For Dissent in their famous *History* (1808), are content to list their conscientious objections to a state church in a manner familiar to Calamy and others a hundred years previously, to ignore the second class citizenship which this entailed, to plead rather for moderation and charity between Christians, to express general satisfaction with the balance of the constitution, and to bask in the equilibrium established by the Glorious Revolution of 1688. A philosophy as negative, historic and non-assertive as this, it may be ventured, suggested itself naturally to the doctors, lawyers, merchants, teachers and their ministerial confrères whose power base was the capital and who dwelt on terms of familiarity with representatives of the established order. (Unhappily, as Ursula Henriques points out,[13] it was precisely this argument based on equilibrium, 'our happy constitution', which the authorities in the decades following the French Revolution were to use *against* the advocates of change. The tables were thus successfully turned against the moderate Dissenters whose intellectual defence crumbled beneath their feet.) This metropolitan phalanx was the Dissenting elite of the day, bland, tolerant and compromising habitués of the coffee houses, not yet seriously challenged or disturbed by the cruder, more abrasive demands of newly rich Dissenting manufacturers from the industrialized Midlands and the North.

This type of tepid Whiggism was not, however, the sole Dissenting attitude in the 1800s. For other representative men, later eighteenth-century religion, whether of the rationalist or revivalist type, both of which spread effectively across denominational barriers, suggested a broad 'catholic' Christianity—indeed Bogue used the phrase himself when hailing the developing friendliness between Arminians and Calvinists: he was attending, he declared, 'the funeral of bigotry'. But 'catholic Christianity' was an ambiguous idea, capable of widely differing interpretations. For Bogue it signified a warm evangelicalism, first enunciated in his particular tradition by Doddridge, and fanned to a flame by the evangelical revival of which his missionary-orientated Gosport Academy was a powerful expression. For others, however, particularly the old Presbyterians of Arian inclination who were in many ways the intellectual cream of both London and provincial Dissent, as such organizations as the Birmingham Lunar Society had clearly proved, catholic Christianity implied a more radical rationale, Baxterian in origin, and leading through the 'middle way' of the eighteenth-century Presbyterians to a loftier religious liberalism, enlightened, philosophic and internationalist. Nor was this posture

---

[13] U. Henriques, *The Development of Religious Toleration in England* (1961), 265.

confined to the Presbyterians: much of the trouble in earlier nineteenth-century Wesleyanism is to be explained by the embarrassing presence in that denomination of an easier liberal tradition represented by such men as Dr Adam Clarke, which may well account for the confessionalist and pastoral reaction sponsored by the Bunting party in the 1820s.[14]

Finally, there were among Nonconformists of the 1800s two further intellectual traditions, one old, one new, both regarded with general disfavour and yet both destined to future prominence. Avowed sectarianism seemed to hark back to the fanaticisms of the Civil War period. It was deplored in an age of enlightenment as introverted and un-accommodating, but it still lingered, particularly among Baptists, whose apologists made no secret of the fact that their distinctive rite drew men apart. In one form or another, with or without the additional bond of believer's baptism, sectarianism was about to revive in circles where severe social dislocation and deprivation, relative or absolute, were daily possibilities.[15]

Among advanced Unitarians, on the other hand, of the Priestley, Belsham, Toulmin variety, sectarianism took on a more aggressive and self-assertive form. In this tradition, drawing once again on historical arguments stretching back at least as far as the Salters Hall debates of 1719, and mediated through Andrew Kippis's *Vindication* (1772), leading apologists already called for an unlimited democracy and complete toleration. They based their plea not on divine election, nor on Dominical teaching, as in the mid-seventeenth century, but on the fact of religious pluralism as a social good in itself. For these men Locke's empiricism and Hartleyan psychology counted for more than scriptural testimony or a shared confessionalism. Here was something radically new —a revolutionary feeling of identity, an internalized apologetic based on self-awareness, rather than a passive acceptance of hard-won liberties. Dissent was now seen as instrumental not to the cause of a heavenly kingdom but to the rallying cries of the American and French Revolutions. And it was this humanized, libertarian creed which in the long run was to prevail over every other, in the ranks of militant Dissent, and within the wider Whig/liberal tradition alike.[16]

By the 1850s Dissenters were calling themselves Nonconformists or Freechurchmen, alternative names to which they took readily after the

[14] B. Semmel, *op. cit.*, 172f; I. Sellers, Adam Clarke and The Eternal Sonship (Wesley Historical Society Lecture, 1975).

[15] This is a useful distinction worked out by the sociologists. For absolute deprivation as a stimulus to sectarianism among the very poor one might cite the Walworth Jumpers, the Shakers of Southeast Lancashire, the Free Thinking Christians of Cranfield and elsewhere, and some of the more extreme Baptists; for relative deprivation among higher income groups one could note in particular the Catholic Apostolic Church: see G. Allan, 'A Theory of Millenialism' in *British Journal of Sociology* xxv (1974).

[16] R. E. Ritchie, 'The Origins of English Radicalism, the Changing Rationals for Dissent' in *Eighteenth Century Studies* vii (2) (1973–4).

Scotch Disruption of 1844. The new nomenclature removed at one sweep the sense of inferiority under which the 'Dissenters' had previously laboured, and was a godsend to the Wesleyans who had longed for a less partisan term than Dissenter to define their special status in the religious world. A confident and heady sense of impending victory pervaded the Nonconformist ranks. Robert Vaughan was triumphantly demonstrating the happy agreement of the Independent polity with the culture of the new cities, J. Baldwin Brown the excellence of the Nonconformist domestic virtues of thrift, family loyalty, self-help and fireside comforts, and their superiority to the depraved tastes of social classes above and below;[17] voluntaryism which Edward Miall equated with 'pure and undefiled religion' seemed set fair to carry all before it. Vital piety may have been less conspicuous in the new 'churches' than in the old 'chapels', moral smugness was a poor substitute for the disciplines of confessionalist theology, public worship less dignified, and preaching more 'practical' and 'direct'. But when even cabinet ministers were beginning to take a note of the Nonconformist demand for retrenchment in finances, a peaceful foreign policy and avoidance of alien entanglements, and to pledge the removal of the remaining Dissenting grievances over church rates, the universities and burials, the Nonconformist could be forgiven for thinking that his 'ethos' was on the verge of triumphing at last. The new *Nonconformist* journal in which Herbert Spencer had written his first essays in philosophic individualism assured him that it was.

Confidence was, however, not absolute, and to the Nonconformist of the 50s nagging doubts pressed down from above and welled up from below. From above, the first generation of Nonconformist gentlemen educated in the new private schools which had developed earlier in the century alongside the theological colleges, were just beginning to taste the traditional culture of the ruling classes and to find the experience refreshing. Educated Unitarians and Congregationals learnt from their learned journals, *The Prospective* and *The British Quarterly Review*, of contemporary trends of thought, in theology, philosophy, politics, fiction even. Taste in the arts and aesthetic pleasure were now being actively pursued in refined Nonconformist households and not least in the theological colleges, in the Unitarians' at York under Charles Wellbeloved, in the Congregationals' at Cheshunt under J. R. Reynolds. Unitarians recognized that their 'quaternion' of intellectuals, Martineau, Tayler, Beard and Wicksteed were taken notice of (and rightly so) by the world of learning; Congregationals felt with less justification the same about their own Baldwin Brown, Vaughan and Paxton Hood. Even the Baptists had their solitary essayist, John Foster, the eccentric misanthrope whom a succession of disastrous pastorates had driven to take up the profession

---

[17] R. Vaughan, *The Age of Great Cities* (1843); J. Baldwin Brown, *The Divine Life in Man* (1860); *The Home Life* (1866).

of letters and who was now hailed as the intellectual ornament of the body.

Clever Nonconformist literati could even afford the luxury of criticizing the brashness and materialism of the 1851 Exhibition, or like the Unitarian Rathbones or the Congregationals Binney and Reynolds, of cultivating the friendship of Matthew Arnold whose notorious attacks on the Philistines still lay twenty years ahead. In the metaphorical conceit of the day Hellenism seemed to be triumphing over Hebraism at last.[18] Fortunately, few Nonconformist heads were as yet turned completely in consequence of these liberating experiences: Henry Allon, who felt that young men should acquire knowledge of doubt from the best pagan literature for 'Christianity would not do everything', was as yet exceptional.

From below came other alarms to shake the bland assurance of the mid-nineteenth century Nonconformist world. Edward Miall's painful analysis of the divisions in society and in the churches, his attacks on the 'trade spirit', social snobbery, materialism and the alienation of the labouring from the professional classes, first delivered to the Congregational Union in 1848, and repeated in his remarkable *British Churches In Relation To The British People* (1849) began a heated and guilt-ridden debate in Congregationalism and in the wider Nonconformist world which culminated fruitfully in Andrew Mearns's *Bitter Cry of Outcast London* (1883) and less happily in the suggestion of Joshua Wilson for the provision of 'one plain, simple and commodious building' in each city for the worshipping needs of 'that most interesting class—the workingmen and their families'. The 1848 revolutions, as the elaborate comments in their journals make clear, had considerably alarmed the Nonconformists[19] and the 1851 census, when properly evaluated, had not assuaged their fears. Henceforth the social problem was to be added to the complex of concerns over which these most intense of men agonized in print and in private.

The Nonconformists of the 1890s were hardly less committed than their fathers' generation. More solidly middle-class they may well have been, but their range of concerns had broadened remarkably. Collectivism bulked much larger now in their thinking about themselves and their society. Perhaps it was that the natural 'religious socialism' which Beatrice Webb had observed in the chapel communities of Rossendale was now coming everywhere to the fore; certainly their increasing acquaintance with the realities of politics and especially their temperance commitment had led them to surprising breaches of laissez faire, especially when it came to the question of appropriating or compensating

---

[18] This distinction is worked out most convincingly by C. Binfield in his 'Thomas Binney and Congregationalism's Special Mission' in *CHST* xxi (1) (1971).

[19] In the Unitarian *Inquirer* for example events in France and elsewhere crowded out all other news between February and July 1848.

for 'property in vice'. But here, as has been noted already, Non-conformists were moving in step with their mentors, particularly T. H. Green.

Social concern may also, as Inglis suggests, have been the natural complement of a developing religious liberalism.[20] With Congregation-als and Baptists, this seems particularly true in the case of clerical leaders such as J. B. Paton, R. F. Horton, C. F. Aked, and John Clifford, and of laymen like the extraordinary Congregational manu-facturer, F. W. Crossley, who dedicated himself to a life of unstinting social service in the slums of Ancoats. The equation is, however, less certain in the case of the Wesleyans: though true enough in respect of H. P. Hughes, it seems rather to have been his broad education at London University which drove Scott Lidgett to espouse a collecti-vist creed in *The Fatherhood of God* (1902), and wide reading in secular literature which produced the remarkable socialism of Samuel Keeble, a thoroughly orthodox evangelical, whose *Industrial Daydreams* (1896) and short-lived *Methodist Weekly* mark the emergence of a significant movement towards Christian socialism in the Wesleyan body.

Darwin, too, played his part in blunting the cutting edge of Non-conformist individualism. From the initial reactions to the *Origin of Species* (learned appreciation and welcome on the part of Unitarians, characteristically obtuse claims by the Methodist New Connexion and others that Darwin was merely revealing a few more examples of divine wisdom in creation, bewilderment and confusion among the humbler Methodist sects, fierce denunciation by Baptists of the stricter sort) the conviction had gradually set in that the struggle for survival could by an idealistic leap be transmuted into a struggle for the life of others—a feat of intellectual self-deception which Nonconformists shared with some of the leading minds of the time. Yet few can doubt the profound impact of a scientific evolutionism christianised in the manner of Professor Drummond on the Nonconformist thinking of the 90s. For every minister who felt impelled to write a book on the subject, such as E. Griffith Jones, the Congregational, with his influential *Ascent Through Christ* (1899), a hundred others dwelt on the same theme in tracts, sermons and articles, or lived out their creeds in settlements, down-town missions or local politics.

Finally, there was appearing in Nonconformity what the sensitive Unitarian William Rathbone called a 'satiety of civilization'[21], a nagging discontent with that very quality of life which the Noncon-formist apologists of fifty years before had apostrophized. Ministers were particularly affected: it was his experience with the superficial materialism of his solidly bourgeois churches at Surbiton Park and

---

[20] K. S. Inglis, 'English Nonconformity and Social Reform, 1880–1900' in *Past and Present* 13 (1958).
[21] See I. Sellers, 'The Pro-Boer Movement in Liverpool' in *TUHS* xii (2) (1960).

Bowdon Downs which drove the Reverend Alexander Mackennal to his collectivist stand in late Victorian Manchester.[22]

Collectivism was, however, both diminished by a lingering individualism and intensified by other social currents in surprising directions. Egalitarian democracy, as we have seen, was now running riot in the day-to-day life of the churches, and the absolute right of the individual to make or unmake himself a church member was being loudly upheld. Alongside the contemporary Baptist endeavours of Dawson Burns and other to interpret believer's baptism as a social rite, the requisite insignia of the radical reformer, and behind the presentation of the sacrament of the Lord's Supper in the light of the quest for social justice as in the Congregational symposium, *Eden and Gethsemane* (Manchester 1903), the old individualism lingered on more doggedly than ever. Indeed the greater the social commitment, the more pronounced it often seems to be, and the contradictions inherent in the thought of men of R. W. Dale's stature were magnified considerably among lesser men.

Thus the R. J. Campbell who could confidently proclaim that 'there is no such thing as an individual salvation, and no such thing as a lonely or hopeless hell' could nevertheless be extremely individualistic when expounding a favourite theme such as 'the divine sonship—the divine life in every soul of man', or when sternly upbraiding what he was pleased to call 'the average businessman' in his 'assembly'. Likewise Nonconformist manufacturers such as Lord Leverhulme or Seebohm Rowntree could preserve a highly individualistic ethic in their commercial relationships while proving themselves exceptionally generous and farsighted in the social sphere. For the Congregational Halley Stewart indeed the dichotomy was particularly pronounced, from a patronizing of the infant Labour movement on the one hand to a merciless laissez-faire in personal and family relations on the other.[23]

There is finally present in the Nonconformist mentality of the 1890s a stridency, militaristic and imperialistic, hitherto unexperienced save by the Wesleyans by whom it may well have been communicated to the rest[24] and which clashed bitterly with the older pacifist Little England traditions in both the Liberal Unionist eruption of 1886 and in the different attitudes adopted towards the Boer War at the turn of the century. The rise of Nonconformist militarism[25] is a strange phenomenon, with roots in the popularity of the Baptist General Havelock in the Indian Mutiny (which sent the Dissenters' erstwhile pacifism reeling), in the successful campaign of W. H. Rule to secure government

[22] D. Macfadyen, *A. Mackennal* (1905) 166f.
[23] See further J. H. S. Kent, 'Hugh Price Hughes and The Nonconformist Conscience in *Essays in Modern History In Memory of Norman Sykes* (1966).
[24] As early as 1836 the Reverend J. R. Stephens had seen in Wesleyanism the most powerful agency for the advancement of the British Empire.
[25] O. Anderson, 'The Growth of Christian Militarism In Mid-Victorian Britain' in *EHR* lxxxvi (1971).

recognition for Wesleyan army chaplains in the 1860s, through what Olive Anderson has called the 'guerilla cult' of the 60s and 70s, Boys Brigades, Shoeblack Brigades, the Salvation Army itself, the quasi-military hymnology and imagery of the Moody-Sankey revival to the full-blown social imperialism of the 1890s. 'Christian Imperial-lism' Hughes and the Liberal Imperialists among the Wesleyans chose to call it, 'God's Greater Britain' was the vision of John Clifford, a more surprising convert to the cult. Kiplingesque contradictions somehow struck a sympathetic chord in Nonconformist minds, and perhaps the greatest paradox of all is that Hughes, Clifford and those Non-conformists who had espoused most completely the imperialist creed should have been the loudest of all in their vituperation of the Estab-lished Church. Far from presenting the united front of the Free Church Federalists' dreams, Nonconformity entered the new century more hopelessly divided emotionally and ideologically than ever before.

5 Politics

Before Victoria

From 1787–90 Dissenters, whatever their theological complexion, had been united in a fellowship of activity—committees, petitions and agitations for the repeal of the Test and Corporation Acts, and the final attainment of those civic blessings only partially realized by the Glorious Revolution of 1688. Thereafter with the Anti-Jacobin reaction, their fellowship became one of apprehension and actual suffering: the Priestley riots of 1791 and the trial of the Scots Unitarian reformers of 1793 were but the highlights of a general discomfiture. Those Yorkshire Quakers imprisoned for non-payment of tithes in 1795 in such circumstances that one of them died, or William Winterbotham, the unfortunate West Country Baptist whose similar sufferings in the late 90s contributed a new chapter to Dissenting martyrology, must all have wondered whether the clock had not been put back a century or more. The more advanced and more affluent joined Priestley in flight to America, the rest abandoned the politics of protest altogether, glad enough that at least their chapels remained unscathed and their worship uninterrupted.

But that even this grudging toleration was regarded as excessive in government circles was made clear in 1800 when the Pitt administration, frightened by the success of itinerancy, was only prevented by Irish distractions, the pressure of Anglican Evangelicals and the resolve of high-minded clergymen that internal reform was worthier of the Establishment than the suppression of its Dissenting rivals, from repealing the Toleration Act, on which Dissent's very existence hinged. Toleration, as Professor Ward has reminded us, was in 1800 preserved by a whisker.[1]

The response of Dissenters was predictable: 'no politics' or the most fervent attachment to the principles of 1688 were trumpeted loudly, even when reforming confidence was temporarily revived with the advent of the Grenville administration in 1806 and a number of radical Dissenters like William Roscoe of Liverpool were elected to the short-lived Parliament which abolished the slave trade and toyed with the idea of amending much else. Some Dissenters in fact were even suspected of

[1] W. R. Ward, op. cit., 52.

fawning, the Wesleyans naturally with their traditional attachment to the Established Church, Congregationals such as John Clayton of King's Weigh House Chapel whose very conservative *Duty of Christians To Magistrates* (1791) drew an angry reply from Robert Hall, Baptists like Samuel Fisher, author of *The Duty of Subjects To The Civil Magistrates* (1794) or John Martin of Keppel Street chapel who ran the Regium Donum from 1795 to 1806 and was widely believed to be in government pay (as also were the Presbyterian Abraham Rees and the whole Dissenting fraternity which furtively administered these and allied funds which have been dubbed by a recent historian 'the Dissenters' own system of social security'.[2])

It was the government's knowledge that Dissent would probably betray itself from within which gave rise to the renewed attempt at crushing itinerancy in 1811, led this time by Lord Sidmouth and encouraged by the authorities panicking at the Luddite disturbances in the Midlands and the North. But more mistakenly than in 1800 the government both exaggerated the forces of coercion it could summon to its aid and underestimated the strength of a revived Nonconformity which could no longer be viewed like the eighteenth-century Dissenting Interest as a fairly harmless political pawn. The emotional and unstable Wesleyans, Drs Coke and Clarke whom Sidmouth considered he had won to his side, proved totally unrepresentative of a Methodism which mobilized the whole of its ecclesiastical machinery against the threatened bill, sanctioned an outcrop of provincial agitations, in Manchester and Durham especially, and, most ominously of all, cooperated closely with the older Dissent, particularly with the formidable pressure group, the Protestant Society, founded by John Wilks in 1811. A spate of activity and a shoal of petitions not merely caused the bill to be dropped, but secured the passage of the Little Toleration Act in the more favourable political climate of 1812, to be followed by the long-awaited legalization of Unitarian Dissent the following year.

During the post-war depression it was the Unitarians and Quakers who once again took the lead in Dissenting political activity. Unitarians had grievances additional to those of other Dissenters, not least the enforced trinitarian marriage formula, and were being coerced into ever more radical attitudes by the growing hostility of orthodox Dissenters over local disputes as to the ownership of chapels, notably that at Wolverhampton (1816→) and over the practice of sceptics such as Carlile pleading the act of 1813 in defence of their attacks on orthodox Christianity. The Unitarians were discovering also a kinship with Roman Catholics as fellow sufferers under the penal codes, and in 1819 formed their own society for the redress of grievances on a basis far broader than Wilks's where Orangist sentiments were openly displayed. The Quakers on the other hand worked, as usual, less ostentatiously but equally effectively towards the politicizing of

<hr />

[2] K. R. M. Short, 'The English Regium Donum' in *EHR* lxxxiv (1969), 62.

Dissenting principles. In William Allen's Poor Law activities, Elizabeth Fry's penal reform crusade and Tregelles's Peace movement of 1816 Friends were developing those propagandist techniques of mass petitioning, lobbying, drawing up voting lists and obtaining pledges which they were later to use so effectively in their anti-slavery campaigns. The renewed struggle for religious equality could not be long delayed.

Toleration came of course with the repeal of the Test and Corporation Acts in 1828, which Dissenters saw as a victory for a sustained campaign of pressure from without, and a vindication of the idea of toleration for which they had always contended. But in arguing like this the Dissenters were deceiving both themselves and others. As Ursula Henriques has shown,[3] the theory of toleration was by this time displaying less vitality than it had in the 1780s partly because the Dissenters no longer agreed among themselves how best to support it, partly because the argument from 'natural rights' no longer carried much weight in a cultural milieu predisposed to Benthamite determinism, partly because the Dissenting apologetic so painfully worked out over the years had by now been taken over by the Whigs, the Benthamites themselves and even by Coleridgean Tories who drew from it precisely the opposite conclusions from those which its erstwhile champions desired.

As for the pressure groups, spectacular local successes, such as the capture of the Sheffield vestry, and the virtual ending of the church rate levy there in 1824, should not disguise the fact that a similar coup at Westminster was quite out of the question. For one thing, Dissenters could not speak with a united voice.[4] The Unitarian and Protestant Societies could not conceal the fact that their widely divergent attitudes to Catholic emancipation made a united effort for the redress of their own grievances impossible—which is what Halévy meant when he wrote that it was doctrinal differences among the Dissenters which delayed the achievement of emancipation. Somewhere in the centre stood the august London 'interest' groups, the Body and the Deputies, wily and compromising as ever, but spurred into a more militant stance by outside pressures after 1826, whilst in Parliament itself William Smith M.P., the Dissenters' champion, was prepared to wait for the favourable political moment and then resort to tactical manoeuvering in order to secure repeal: he was apprehensive about external agitation which he rightly saw as counter-productive. And there was certainly yet another interested group, Dissenting ministers and laymen who were very tepid reformers, the Claytons, Raffles of Liverpool, Jay of Bath, Vaughan of Manchester, constitutionalists not revolutionaries, prepared to leave it to the Whigs. It is the presence of these men which

---

[3] U. Henriques, *op. cit.*, 262.
[4] See R. W. Davis, 'The Strategy of Dissent in The Repeal Campaign, 1820–28' in *Journal of Modern History* xxxviii (1966); *idem, Dissent In Politics. The Political Life of William Smith MP* (1971), 102f.

serves as a warning not to interpret, with J. H. Hexter, the dissenting rivalries of the 20s as a social clash between high-born London enlightenment and uncouth northern bigotry, or 1828 as a final sell-out of Dissenting 'interest politics' to provincial militancy.[5]

Of all the interested parties, William Smith alone had hit upon the correct tactic. While old Tories disliked repeal because it would let in Catholic Emancipation, 'Catholic' Tories because once granted it would harden opinion against emancipation, and Whigs because it was a tiresome diversion from the emancipation which was their chief political goal, the redress of Dissenting grievances stood no chance. It was a last minute tactical shift on the part of Lord Russell who decided to concede repeal as a means of weakening the forces ranged against emancipation which really carried the day in the Dissenters' favour.

But the fact that at the last minute the Dissenting groups had with extreme difficulty and much wrangling formed a common front (known as the United Committee) enabled them to hail Repeal as a great victory for their own militancy. A powerful myth was thus born which was to be applied to every governmental concession in their favour throughout the next fifty years.

The return of the Whigs in 1830 and the Reform Bill of 1832 raised Dissenting temperatures to boiling point. Brougham and Wellington from opposite points of view considered that a large new body of wealthy and intelligent electors would transform the political scene: Dissent had ceased to be a negative interest and had become a political phenomenon of startling potential. Yet, however great Dissenting influence in the constituencies, the actual number of Nonconformists returned to the reformed House of Commons was less than a dozen, and half of these were Unitarians: certainly its parliamentary representation bore no relationship to the impressive Nonconformist strength talked about confidently by Lord Grey and local Dissenting leaders a few months previously when the swamping of the Lords with Whig peers was being planned in detail.

In some confusion the Deputies combined with others to form a United Committee in March 1833 to press for a programme of reforms which was enlarged to embrace disestablishment of the Church of England fourteen months later. But first a lingering abuse was swept away, to the applause of all Nonconformists, Evangelical and Liberal alike. Slavery was finally abolished in 1833, a belated victory for the Quaker/Unitarian propaganda machine, reinforced latterly by a phalanx of orthodox Dissenters, by William Knibb, the Baptist platform orator, fresh from his personal experiences in the West Indies, by Congregationals still agitated by the martyrdom of John Smith, their Demerara missionary in 1823, by Wesleyans who had by now 23,000 slave members in the West Indies, and whose leaders Coke and

---

[5] J. H. Hexter, 'The Protestant Revival and The Catholic Question in England' in *Journal of Modern History* viii (1936).

Watson were prominent in the final stages of the agitation, and by a notable Presbyterian layman, Mr William Thompson.

On the home front however, Grey and Melbourne disappointed.[6] Dissenters were chagrined by the politicians' failure to push through University Test and Marriage Law emendations in 1834, as well as by their temporizing over church rates. The *Eclectic Review* in fact found the Poor Law Amendment Act to have been the only 'redeeming' feature of an unproductive session. The brief return of Peel (1834–35) troubled the Dissenters in an unexpected way, for there was none of the anticipated reversion to overt reaction: rather the Ecclesiastical Commission proved unexceptionably active and blunted the cutting edge of the Dissenters' attack. In a fright Nonconformity patched up its alliance with the Whigs and a Parliamentary Committee was formed in 1835 with branches in the provinces to secure the return of Dissenting or at least pro-Dissenting MPs. The Municipal Corporations Act (the statute most obviously advantageous to Protestant Dissent since the repeal of 1828), the Marriage and Tithe Bills, Civil Registration and the new Charter for London University all gave satisfaction to some degree.

But the ending of burdensome penal legislation only threw into relief the irksome restrictions which remained, and the failure of the Church Rates Bill, killed eventually not so much by episcopal opposition as by the hostility of Whig gentry in the House of Commons, marked a new phase of Dissenting disenchantment with their political champions. In 1837, the year following the foundation of the Church Rates Abolition Society and the year also when the radical Dr Price took over from the moderate Eustace Conder as editor of the *Eclectic*, Dissenters worked out a much more radical and extremist programme. Independent political initiatives were essayed, especially by the orthodox Dissenters, in the General Election of that year, yet total Dissenting representation was hardly increased and Baines was the only Congregational to be elected. Once again, as throughout the 30s a few spectacular achievements were chalked up, not so much at the expense of the Tories, who secretly benefitted from Nonconformist go-it-alone tactics, as of mild Whigs or secular Radicals. The 30s thus ended on a sour note: Dissenting fanaticism had driven Whigs like Russell and Melbourne into an erastianism more unyielding and suspicious than ever, a reviving Tory sentiment had emasculated Bougham's 1839 education scheme which Dissenters, the Wesleyans excepted, had approved with a few reservations, the new-fangled voluntaryism appeared in Parliament and the provinces so wholly unreasonable and factional that it seemed, in the words of Professor Gash, more like 'a retreat from politics' altogether.[7] In 1841, the year of the Whig eclipse,

[6] See further N. Gash, *Reaction and Reconstruction In English Politics, 1832–52* (1965), 66f.

[7] N. Gash, *op. cit.*, 76.

Miall in his *Nonconformist's Sketchbook* described Dissent as a disbanded army, without discipline, respected and feared by no one.[8]

For this state of affairs Dissenters had only themselves to blame. In the first place they were by now chronically weakened by their own divisions.[9] Relations between Unitarians and the Orthodox had deteriorated sharply since the Manchester Unitarian Controversy of 1825, the Baptist Joseph Ivimey had since 1829 waged continuous war against the Unitarian hold on Dr Williams Library and Trust, the Dissenting Deputies and the General Body of Protestant Ministers. Gradually Baptist and Congregational opinion had hardened in his favour, and further contentions over the Lady Hewley Charity as well as the growing influence of orthodox Scots Presbyterians completed the Unitarians' discomfiture. The result was a dramatic split in both the General Body and the Deputies in 1836, and the dislodgement of the heterodox. (The assertive political leadership of the Unitarian elite and their liberal theology seem to have occasioned an equal amount of rancour). Now orthodox Dissenters who worked with Unitarians in any capacity (and there were a few still associated with the unsavoury Regium Donum) risked dark comparisons with Herod or Pilate in the denominational magazines. Their foes in the Establishment rejoiced at these Dissenting splits, and recovered their composure: Gladstone's *Essay on Church and State* (1838) is symptomatic of the Church's reviving self-confidence.

Even within politically-conscious Dissent there were still varying degrees of activism ranging from the intense to the indifferent. Joseph Conder's newspaper, *The Patriot* (founded 1832) took a moderate, constitutional, Whiggish line, Price's *Eclectic* was far more single-mindedly voluntaryist, while the Unitarian *Christian Reformer* was already developing a zeal for state-financed and secular education and a dislike for voluntaryism of most kinds. (This dislike was, even as early as the 1830s, widespread in places like Birmingham where the Church Rates issue had been decided in 1832, and relations between Nonconformists and Anglicans had settled down to a nodding acquaintance-ship.) In truth the Dissenters of the 30s had none of the advantages which were to be theirs a decade later: no firebrand like Miall, no militant journal like the *Nonconformist*, no electoral organization like that of 1847. As late as 1832 the *Eclectic* doubted whether the majority of Dissenters really objected to the Establishment as such, and Robert Vaughan confessed in 1838 that however desirable voluntaryism might be in theory, in practice it would have to be postponed as the Church was still too powerful, especially in the countryside. It was this kind of unsureness and feeling of inferiority which Anglicans throughout

---

[8] E. Miall, *The Nonconformists' Sketchbook* (1842), 5.
[9] K. R. M. Short, 'London's General Body of Protestant Ministers. Its Disruption in 1836' in *J Ecc H* xxlv (4) (1973).

the 1830s seized upon in order to hail the 'pious' Dissenters as still the exponents of majority Nonconformist opinion, and Political Dissent as the creed of an ugly minority of malcontents. In contrast to the gigantic polemics of later decades their judgement seems in retrospect shrewd and balanced.

Early and mid Victorian

The great meeting of Dissenting ministers engineered by the Anti-Corn Law League in 1841 as part of its propaganda campaign marked, according to Guiness Rogers, 'the starting point in the public life of the Free Churches'. This, however, appears to be yet another example of late Victorian Nonconformist myth-making. The campaign was, both in personnel and in the arguments employed, very much a continuation of the abolitionist agitation and concern over the West Indian apprenticeship system which had agitated Dissenters, particularly Baptists, in the later 1830s. Dissenting ministers discerned in the early 40s a causal link between the survival of the Corn Laws in Britain and of Slavery in the American South, and it was on this sentiment that the Leaguers deliberately played. The ministers like the middle-class ladies in their tea-meetings were undoubtedly being 'used' (made 'instrumental' as Cobden put it), but were gratified by the unaccustomed approving publicity they now received.[10] Meanwhile in Birmingham there was emerging Joseph Sturge's Complete Suffrage Union, a revamping of those Political Unions of 1830–32 often led by Dissenters like Parkes and Potter, and flourishing in places where the social gulf between middle and working classes was comparatively slight. Whether the CSU drove a wedge into working class/Chartist solidarity or whether it dissipated middle-class energies which should, according to Cobden, have been concentrated on the single issue of the Corn Laws must remain a moot point. Probably the latter: the continuing rates agitation (rate levies were being blocked in fifty-three towns in 1842) must have had a like effect. 'A medley of cross-alignments and secondary issues' is Professor Gash's summing up of the Dissenting campaigns of the early 40s.

But the Dissenters' new-found strength was dramatically put to the test in 1843 when Graham introduced his ill-fated Factory Bill whose education clauses portended an Anglican monopoly over the schooling of factory children.[11] Dissenting ire knew no bounds. Not only was the government compelled to abandon the Bill, largely through the Wesleyans unwontedly throwing their support behind the rest of Nonconformity, but at a great educational conference held in the

[10] K. R. M. Short, 'Baptists and the Corn Laws' in *BQ* xxi (7) (1966).
[11] J. T. Ward and J. H. Treble, 'Religion and Education in 1843: Reaction To The Factory Education Bill' in *J Ecc H* xx (1969), 79f.

Congregational Library in December 1843, the term 'voluntaryism' was coined by Dr James Matheson, and a campaign for disestablishment formally got under way. Miall's Anti-State Church Association emerged the following year.

Dissenters were now too excited to pay much attention to Lord Shaftesbury who shrewdly observed that the defeat of 1843 marked the limits of what Dissenters and Anglicans could both achieve: each had their spheres of influence and neither could henceforth gain ground at the expense of the other. (Professor Best refers to this as 'a kind of self-acting principle of equilibrium', the reality which underlines all the claims and counterclaims of the next fifty years and more.)[12]

The Disestablishment campaign was launched with sound and fury, and was propagandized through a rash of new journals which appeared about the same date. Among the Baptists for example, more unitedly in the van of Dissenting radicalism than the Congregationals, *The Church* first appeared in 1844, *The Baptist Examiner* the same year—both were associated with Dr Benjamin Evans, minister at Scarborough. The platform was vast: Corn Law repeal, Church Disestablishment, Suffrage extension, and Voluntaryism, interpreted as Nonconformist determination to provide their own denominational schools to remedy the deficiencies of existing provision. (The Congregational Board of Education was set up the same year.) Yet even now Dissent could not speak with a single voice. Voluntaryism's aim was officially described as entirely spiritual ('pure and undefiled religion')—which led Dr Price of the *Eclectic* to doubt whether it was political enough, while Vaughan and the *British Quarterly Review* supported by Binney were even now calling for a national secular system as an alternative to suicidal competition among the sects. The Maynooth Grant agitation of the following year underlined again Dissenting splits and Dissenting isolation.[13] Here was another opportunity for the forces of popular Protestantism to show their true strength, for the Wesleyans who in some cases mediated them were now lined up solidly behind the Dissenting opponents of the Grant. But the recent formation of the Evangelical Alliance and renewed cooperation between Evangelical Dissenters and Anglicans threw Nonconformist politics into total confusion: Blackburn of the *Congregational Magazine* and his supporters were prepared to fight shoulder-to-shoulder with Low Church Anglicans, extremists like Miall and *The Nonconformist* readership insisted on keeping their Dissenting purity intact. Meanwhile Whigs and Radicals like Cobden and Hume who voted for the Grant spurned the anti-Maynooth agitation as a Dissenting crotchet. In retaliation Dissenting

---

[12] See G. Best, *op. cit.*, 228ff, and also G. Kitson Clark, *The Making of Victorian England* (1962), 145ff.
[13] G. I. T. Machin, 'The Maynooth Grant, The Dissenters and Disestablishment, 1845–47' in *EHR* lxxxii (1967).

militants decided that the time had come for a complete break with existing party entanglements: they had come of age; they would henceforth walk alone.

Excitement over Corn Law repeal delayed for a year the implementation of this resolve, but in 1846 Russell's education scheme, which aimed at improving the standards of pupil teachers but was suspected of being another Anglican plot, provided an opportunity for concerted action. To counter the effects of this sinister measure a Dissenting Electoral Committee was formed to contest the 1847 General Election purely on the voluntaryist issue. A specific, unaligned and determined Nonconformist party had at last emerged. The result was not quite the hopeless failure Halévy and others imagined it to have been: twenty-six Voluntaryists were returned and another sixty pledged to resist further extension of state-endowed religion. Yet the Dissenters had, as Professor Gash says, succeeded not only in making the election incredibly confused, and securing the defeat of men such as Roebuck and Macaulay, but also in exhibiting themselves as political amateurs and meddlers of the worst kind, still exhibiting the marks of second-class citizenship, their 'inherited handicap', skilled in hostile agitation and obstruction but in constructive politics pitifully inadequate.[14] Their bungling may even have damaged irreparably the whole middle-class political effort, and foreshadowed the later secular failure of Cobden and Bright. They had even forfeited the all-important sympathy of the Wesleyans whom Russell had persuaded to return to the old paths. The result was thus predictable: the government went ahead with its educational grants scheme, the Wesleyan schools were officially recognized and received a government grant, 80 per cent of public monies were attigned to the National Schools, and the British and Foreign Schools Society fell hopelessly behind.

In politics as in much else the 50s and early 60s were a period of inconsequence and further dissipation of efforts into a myriad of different causes. Government in an uncontentious and conciliatory climate could afford to make some generous gestures: the House of Lords decision in the Braintree Church Rates Case (1852), that a rate levied by a minority of vestrymen was henceforth illegal, caused a marked decline in anti-rate agitation and by removing a considerable grievance made the attainment of other Dissenting objectives yet more remote. The Regium Donum, a stumbling block within the Dissenting fraternity rather than a continuing insult to the whole body, finally disappeared in 1851, a bill of 1856 got rid of the more obnoxious features of the 1836 Marriage Act, and legislation of 1847 and 1857 eased the burials situation in the towns though not in the countryside.

Meanwhile the Liberation Society (the name assumed by the Anti-state Church Association in 1855) continued its propaganda exercise. It had enjoyed some success in the General Election of 1852 with the

[14] N. Gash, *op. cit.*, 107.

return of thirty-eight Dissenters. A Parliamentary Committee (Samuel Morley chairman) was set up the following year, and 'whipping' introduced into the Commons, Sir Charles Douglas being the Liberationists' choice as their Whip. A temporary setback during the Crimean War, when Dissenting politics were not in favour with the electorate, was followed by an outburst of activity in 1857. The Society *may* have brought about the fall of Palmerston in that year: it was certainly responsible for a number of Liberal successes, mainly in the counties, and for a number of spectacular Liberal defeats, including Miall's own. Palmerston's stubborn resistance to Liberationist claims, the rejection of yet another Church Rates Bill in 1861 and a nasty brush with the Whig leaders in 1863 led in the General Election of 1865 to a repetition of the tactics of 1847. But this time their efforts, even if they led to the defeat of negligent Liberals by Tories, were by skilful propaganda turned into Liberationist successes. The Society began to boast of itself as the backbone of the Liberal Party, and with eighty-seven Nonconformists returned to Parliament the claim seemed to be well founded.[15]

Throughout the 50s the Liberationists had of course to compete for the favours of the Dissenting laity with a number of other bodies, the Administrative Reform Association (pioneered by young Liverpool Unitarians), C. D. Collet's agitation against the taxes on knowledge and Whitechurst's Ballot Society where Dissenters were again prominent, the Peace Society of which the redoubtable Henry Richard became secretary in 1848, and the United Kingdom Alliance of 1853.

This last was probably the most likely medium for provincial Dissenters to exchange what Brian Harrison has called 'a psychology of persecution' for one of 'dominance', yet the political ineptitude of the Alliance, and the narrowness, inexperience, defiant posturing and occasional hysteria of its supporters, their consciousness of being 'outsiders' ranged against a monstrous system, is highlighted by the Alliance's favourite panacea, the Permissive Bill, 'a symbol rather than a serious proposal for solving the drink problem: it publicly asserted the worth of a distinct culture and eased the consciences of those who felt alarmed at the extent to which the surrounding society either ignored or despised that culture.'[16] Harrison's judgement applies to more than one of the Dissenting crusades of the mid-century.

Were all the Nonconformist political activists so naive? Was none of them able to translate the politics of defiance into those of constructive reform? A glance at their two front rank political leaders, the supporting phalanx of Nonconformist businessmen—politicians, and the constituency shock-troops, the provincial Dissenters who transformed somnolent Whiggism into the new Liberal Party, reveals a range of surprising contrasts.

[15] D. M. Thompson, 'The Liberation Society, 1844–68' in P. Hollis ed., *Pressure From Without* (1974), 225.
[16] B. Harrison, *Drink and The Victorians*, 383.

John Bright and Edward Baines junior stood in very different relationships to the Dissenting world of their day. The Quaker Bright was the most prominent Dissenter in politics, yet was linked to political Nonconformity by the slenderest of threads. What Professor Vincent calls his 'old-fashioned moralism' and his ready acceptance of the secular disciplines of the Manchester School[17] might have been just acceptable to militant Dissent: his laissez-faire hostility to government interference on the slavery issue, on drink, and above all on the disestablishment of the Irish Church (his fears about the threat of disendowment to proprietary rights counted for much here) were as mistrusted as his secularist attitude to education (he had abandoned voluntaryism as early as 1854). None of the Dissenting enthusiasms of the day elicited his support: the Liberation, Peace and Temperance movements sought his championship in vain. Perhaps his immersion in politics at the highest level had opened his eyes to the fatuities of much Dissenting militancy. He still, however, retained enough respect among Liberal Cabinet ministers, Dissenting activists and the populace at large whose suffragist passions he had sought to arouse in the mid-60s, to have been able to hold the three together even after the education and other crises of the early 70s, had not crippling illness tragically supervened.

Baines, unlike Bright, did for a time embrace political Dissent with enthusiasm—and burnt his fingers badly thereby. Having inherited a good measure of political acumen from his father, Baines was at first a good constitutional Whig, anxious to retain the support of the Whig magnates and gentry of Yorkshire and fighting shy of the aggressively middle-class politics of the Anti-Corn Law League. It was the abortive Factory Bill of 1843 which turned his head. Now Dissenting polemic conquered every political scruple and instinct for compromise. By 1847 he had displaced Miall as the leader of organized Dissent and personally led his followers to the debacle of 1847. Voluntaryism was now his chief concern, and the breach with Cobden was complete. (It was no accident that by way of reaction to these Yorkshire antics Cobden made Manchester the centre of movements such as the Lancashire Public School Association for extending state control over education.) Disenchantment with his role as the national conscience of Nonconformity came with the failure of the school building programme of his own Congregational denomination, and the damaging revelations of the Taunton Commission of which he was a member. In 1867 he both abandoned voluntaryism and accepted household suffrage. But in the great radical awakening of 1866–67 he was no leader, rather he was swept along by the tide. Thanks to his twenty years in the Dissenting

---

[17] J. Vincent, *The Formation of the Liberal Party* (Penguin ed. 1972), 221. This attitude should probably be understood in the light of what Mrs Isichei has to say about traditional Quaker fears of striking violent political attitudes, and their inbred talent for ingratiating themselves with the great; Isichei, *Victorian Quakers* (1970), 191f.

wilderness his leadership, as Dr Thompson shewdly observes, 'had become redundant'.[18]

The political stature of Bright, Baines, Miall and their sort thus appears somewhat diminished, particularly in the writing of recent historians who have recalled disapprovingly not only their Dissenting crochets but their laissez-faire opposition to factory regulation of all and social reform of most kinds. Yet as their stock has gone down, that of the great nexus of Nonconformist businessmen cum philanthropists cum amateur politicians which dominated much of the social and economic life of mid-Victorian Britain has risen proportionately. These second generation businessmen of whom William Rathbone VI of Liverpool was the chief, their fortunes made, creative and dynamic, both guilt-ridden and resentful of past and present ostracisms, even in an age when class politics had died down, secure, and yet still resistant to the assimilative pull of the class above them, were, according to Professor Vincent, the 'heroic element' in mid-Victorian Liberalism, 'the intransigents of the party, the one group which surprised by a fine excess'.[19]

Extreme individualists, yet tender-minded and with a most active social concern, they provided reinforcement for the Liberal intelligentzia of the 60s whose mouthpiece was the *Fortnightly Review* and excelled in politics by life-long, passionate commitment to some reforming cause, usually organized on a national basis. Thus Rathbone's own agitation for the reform of the Bankruptcy Laws and District Nursing is paralleled by the Ryland's work for the reshaping of the diplomatic service, Stansfeld's campaign for the repeal of the Contagious Diseases Acts, C. D. Collet's for the abolition of the Taxes on Knowledge, Fildes's for the ending of hanging, Peter Taylor's for European nationalism, Dixon's and Read's for national education. Sometimes it was an ephemeral cause which attracted these men: the defence of responsible trade unionism after the Sheffield outrages, the prosecution of Governor Eyre. Sometimes, too, a crusade which *should* have illustrated merely the Dissenting prejudices or mental limitations of these *nouveaux riches* reveals once again the same surprising radical idealism and generosity of sentiment. This appears true of the role of Jupe, Lingford and Emmott in the United Kingdom Alliance, and of Morley and J. I. Travers in the Financial Reform Association. It was almost as if the business genius, philanthropic instinct and political concern of the Quakers, long nourished through their network of interlocking directorships and channelled via their tradition of petitioning to the lawmakers at Westminster, had come to characterize the whole of Nonconformity— indeed not a few of these men, the Rathbones, Crosfields and Reckitts particularly, were themselves ex-Quakers or closely related thereto.

Professor Vincent's very favourable portrait of these Nonconformist

[18] See D. Fraser, 'Edward Baines' in P. Hollis, *op. cit.*, 183f.
[19] J. Vincent, *op. cit.*, 39.

businessmen-politicians of the mid-Victorian decades has not gone unchallenged by some of his critics. Michael Hurst,[20] for example, has questioned firstly whether our Dissenters were driven, as Vincent claims, to these fruitful agitations on the sidelines of politics because their excessive veneration for the principles of 1662 and inability to stand anywhere else than in opposition somehow deprived them of a role at the centre and secondly whether all Nonconformist businessmen were really as enlightened as the above. He cites Sir Titus Salt whose radical idealism at Saltaire did not prevent his originating the National Federation of Associated Employers of Labour, and Joseph Chamberlain's notorious exclusion of Trade Unionism from his factories. But Vincent's thesis, especially when reinforced by a number of local studies, stands up well to his critics: Nonconformists *did* tend to view events through the eyes of their persecuted forebears, while for every business chief who erred on the side of class-motivated cunning, there were others whose radical passions ran to a real excess, the Quaker H. J. Wilson, the Sheffield smelter, F. W. Crossley, the hermit of Ancoats, or James Samuelson, the Liverpool Unitarian businessman turned lawyer who championed trade union rights in the courts.

The generals of political Nonconformity came overwhelmingly from Lancashire and Yorkshire, the troops from small towns, the countryside (the old Cromwellian counties in particular), the Celtic fringe, the coalfields, or, to some extent, London. Popular Dissent was, according to Vincent, only one of three strands, the others being the provincial daily press and a politically awakened artisanry, which coalesced to create the modern Liberal Party, but it was possibly the most significant. The local branches of the Liberation Society took the lead: here the Nonconformist conscience was brought to birth, for Free Religion was seen as complementary to all the other freedoms— particularly Free Trade—while issues such as a just foreign policy, capital punishment and women's rights, the ballot and the franchise were debated earnestly. (On some issues, it is only fair to add—and here the angularities of the Conscience come peeping through— Liberationists were more muted: concessions to Ireland and further doses of social reform were not high on their list of priorities.)

Perhaps, however, the chief significance of the Liberationist and Temperance movements was that they brought to Liberalism not moral fervour but votes and party discipline. It was the national system of agents which the Liberation Society promoted from its seemingly inexhaustible funds, the selection and approving of candidates, the campaigns for the registration of voters, significant in England and all-important in Wales, which provided the model and the personnel for the nascent Liberal Party organization in the provinces. Its campaigns were brilliantly successful—only in Lancashire did its efforts take on a too obviously sectarian character and rebound to the Liberals'

[20] M. Hurst, 'Liberal versus Liberal' in *Historical Journal* xv (4) (1972).

discomfiture. Gladstonian Liberalism could hardly have got off the ground without the dedicated zeal of organized Nonconformity.

Yet even in the 60s, before Gladstone had drawn the teeth of Dissenting militancy, some of its paradoxes and much of its awkwardness and ineffectiveness had become conspicuous. First, it was very much a movement of radical Dissent, Methodist sectarian and Baptist: the more staid Congregationals and particularly the Wesleyans (despite the promptings of Morley Punshon in the early 60s) looked at it askance. Secondly, tensions were bound to develop between London where its headquarters lay, the areas of its popular strength in the Midlands and East Anglia, and the North where its leadership was concentrated. Thirdly, it aged very rapidly after younger Dissenters who had been captivated in large numbers in the 50s lost interest in the following decade, but not before many had made the transition from service to the chapel to absorption in local or national politics, and the Society had itself been invaded by agnostics and secular reformers who seized the opportunity to turn confessional militancy into a more general assault on the Establishment as a social encumbrance. Finally, the chief tragedy of Liberationism was that it constantly found itself overtaken by events. Its influence being strongest in county constituencies and small market towns, its significance was eclipsed by the creation of large urban electorates in 1867 and of large rural ones in 1885, for both of which extensions of the suffrage it had of course been to some extent responsible. There again every concession extorted from Parliament, such as those affecting Ireland and the Colonies and Church Rates in the years 1866–88 somehow made the ultimate goal of Disestablishment more remote than ever. Disraeli proved in the early 60s how easy it was to frustrate the Society by raising the cry 'The Church In Danger', a lesson not lost on Gladstone in his handling of political Dissent. In the last analysis, as D. M. Thompson says, the diffused radicalism and lingering Whiggism of the Liberal Party were always able to emasculate it by a series of small but timely concessions. Brilliant in agitation and bringing questions to public notice (though even here malleable in the hands of more skilled political leaders), its impotence was never more conspicuous than in the House of Commons itself where it beheld with chagrin others taking the political decisions and reaping the political benefits where it had generously sown.[21]

But that political Dissent disguised its frustrations with an exaggerated opinion of its own significance, as contributing 'soul' and 'uplift', 'all that is best' to evolving democracy[22] is made painfully clear

[21] D. M. Thompson in P. Hollis, *op. cit.*, 233f.

[22] As Olive Anderson points out, this belief hardened into a late Victorian myth or cliché, taken for granted by Skeats and Miall in their influential *History* (1891) and by W. B. Selbie in his *Nonconformity* (1912) and still cultivated in Nonconformist circles. See O. Anderson, 'Gladstone's Abolition of Compulsory Church Rates' in *J Ecc H* xxv (2) (1973); K. R. M. Short, 'The English Indemnity Acts' in *Church History* xlii (5) (1973).

by the two measures passed by Parliament in 1867–68, the clearest illustration to date of what Gladstone was privately to dub the Non-conformists' 'Brobdignagian estimates of their Lilliputian proceedings'. The Indemnity Acts were finally swept away in 1867, a measure hailed by Dissenters as a spectacular triumph for the principles of civil and religious liberty. But the Acts had long since ceased to have any practical consequences whatsoever—save in so far as they occasioned abstract and rather arid debates at church meetings on matters of deep principle. Shortly afterwards Church Rates were 'abolished' according to the Liberationists, declared to be no longer enforcable at law and commuted into voluntary payments in legislative reality. Again the measure was widely acclaimed as signalizing a major Dissenting triumph. In fact Church Rates were no longer a live issue in the towns and seldom in the shires, while the real struggle behind the passing of this strange compromise measure was not between the foes and apostles of religious liberty but between Evangelical and Broad Church Anglicans on the one hand and Gladstonian 'voluntaryism' (to his critics a thinly disguised ritualism) on the other.

These stirs are a fitting preamble to the great Gladstone ministry of 1868–74. The disestablishment of the Irish Church (1868) appeared a Nonconformist triumph: to some historians indeed it still symbolizes Gladstone's submission to Dissenting force majeure. The evidence seems to suggest, however, that the Liberationists' actual role in the final stages was very small, and was largely confined under Gladstone's manipulative genius to constraining the Roman Church to accept dis-endowment rather than concurrent endowment. The Prime Minister could thus well afford to congratulate the Society on the moderation displayed throughout the struggle.

There followed the Forster Education Act of 1870. If this bill marks the parting of the ways for secular Liberalism and political Noncon-formity, it should also be recognized that the previous decade had seen a volte-face on the part of Dissent unexampled in its entire history. In the early 60s voluntaryism save among the Wesleyans was at its height: by 1867 its chief apostle Baines was urging the acceptance of government grants for the future, and the Baptist Union was pressing for a secular system. The Unitarians, it appears, had been among the first to abandon voluntaryism: R. W. Dale and his followers veered towards state intervention in their train. The result was the National Education League, founded in Birmingham in 1869 to press for free, compulsory and unsectarian schooling. Old-fashioned evangelicals like Spurgeon who loved the Bible shrank from a fully secular system, just as Shaftes-bury was aghast at F. D. Maurice's educational thinking which had evolved in a manner rather similar to Dale's. But their voices were swamped by the Dissenting clamour which greeted Forster's Act, whose object was to continue, if not perpetuate, the dual system: 'the worst act', Bright described it, 'passed by any Parliament since 1832'. The

Central Nonconformist Committee was formed in March 1870 to rouse opinion against the Act, particularly the hated Clause 25. But all that was secured was the notorious Cowper-Temple amendment concerning the provision and timing of undenominational religious instruction in Board Schools, another opportune concession by government which satisfied enough provincial Dissenters to moderate the force of the campaign and hardened the opposition of the older 'religious' Nonconformists, Spurgeon and Conder, Stoughton and Newman Hall, to the purely secular platform of Dale and Guiness Rogers. Though by the time of the great Manchester meeting in January 1872 organized opposition to the Forster Bill was still running high, and though as late as 1874 a pledge was extorted from 300 out of 425 Liberal candidates to repeal Clause 25, the Liberal leadership had by now gone far towards convincing the voters that the programme of the Education League was little more than a sectarian crotchet.

By this date a coalition of 'all the Leagues', to use Forster's famous phrase, was harrying the government at every turn. Over licensing legislation Gladstone was apparently content to allow the Nonconformists to focus their resentments on what was no more than a symbol: it diverted their attention away from more vital issues. Even so there was joy in Cabinet circles at the Dissenters' falling apart after all the sound and fury of their anti-drink crusade. Some shrank in alarm from the radical solutions such as government taxation of drink or municipal control which their platform seemed to warrant; other, more advanced ones, such as Chamberlain and Cadbury, progressed to just such solutions, while still other prominent leaders, Bright and Baines, Morely, Charles Gilpin and Joseph Curwen, realized astutely just how electorally damaging anti-drink legislation could be, and refused to countenance the follies of the Temperance men. Lawson's Permissive Bill became an annual event, and its overwhelming defeat an equally predictable one.

Thus when the Liberationists prepared themselves for their final onslaught against the Establishment in 1871 they were in a weakened position. Miall, who had clashed seriously with Gladstone over the Forster Bill, had made himself look ridiculous by announcing it had all been 'a lover's quarrel'; Gladstone himself was about to make another of those brilliantly timed concessions, the abolition of University Tests, and had just added Henry Winterbotham, a prominent Nonconformist politician, to his cabinet. The result was that despite a massive propaganda campaign in the provinces, Miall's motion of May 9th was lost, though not as decisively as it was destined to be in future years, when the Liberationists wearied their fellow MPs with their annual motion. Disestablishment joined the Permissive Bill as a Dissenting lost cause.

By this date it had done its divisive worst. Chamberlain, impatient of these fatuities, broke with Miall to formulate his more radical

Unauthorized Programme, Free Schools, Free Land and a Free Church, as he adumbrated it as early as 1872, while the Leagues' constant intervention in by-elections had halved the government's majority by 1873 without noticeable benefit to themselves. In desperation Gladstone, who earlier that year had warmed Dissenting hearts again by the unexpected publication of his pamphlets attacking Papal claims, suddenly dissolved Parliament, and conducted a brief election campaign, hoping thereby to catch his Nonconformist critics unprepared. As far as the Nonconformists, though not of course the wider electorate, were concerned, Gladstone had once again reckoned aright. Of the leading men only Dale remained resolute in hostility, most returned to the Liberal fold, the rest retreated into sullen indifference.

Why had this Nonconformist political endeavour failed so miserably? The narrative of these events of 1868–74 has already revealed some of the causes, but other profounder ones lay beneath the surface of the political debate in Westminster and the provinces. It is clear, for example, that Nonconformist political leaders by this date fell into an assortment of heterogeneous groups: those who like Dale and the Liberationists saw the Liberal Party as a vehicle for promoting Nonconformist interests, even if it was destroyed in the process, those who like Samuel Morley, proprietor of the *Daily News* or J. J. Colman, MP for Norwich, loyally supported the Party even when it went against those interests, those like Jacob Bright, Peter Rylands and Henry Richard who were prepared to be loyal to Gladstone, but never subservient, and a small group of advanced social reformers led by William Fowler, the Quaker MP for Cambridge.

Secondly, it is clear that after 1870 the provincial activists, abandoning Liberal politics in despair, had renewed their attachments to their former loves, the local branches of the Liberation Society, UKA and NEL—with disastrous practical consequences. It was not only politically damaging to the legislative realization of their goals: it had the effect, not lost on the Liberal leadership, of exhibiting All The Leagues as dominated by a small group of middle-aged, if energetic, businessmen, hopelessly overworked and overstretched, and too few in number ever to forge their organizations into anything more menacing than the vexatious pressure groups they undoubtedly were. Finally, it is only too apparent that by 1874 militant Dissent was still fighting the battles of the past—of the 1840s, in fact. When Miall tentatively approached the working-class leaders of the London Working Men's Association and the Reform League in 1871–72 with the suggestion of an accommodation, and George Howell responded with demands for a real and not a subordinate partnership and with plans for a full-blooded programme of social reform to overturn a wider establishment than the Church of England, the Liberationists at once took fright. Their single-minded stress on a 'holy warfare' against 'the one great anti-scriptural system' of the Established Church seemed strangely dated to the radical artisans of the 70s. Not surprisingly, the negotiations broke down, and in the eyes of the working-class leadership the nascent Nonconformist Conscience was shown up as already tinged with the negative disapproving quality of its later years.[23]

Enough of these bitter lessons were learnt by the Nonconformists themselves to convince them in the later 70s that they must sink sectarian politics in the interests of a wider Liberal unity. The UKA was the first to recognise this sobering reality—just after the 1874 election in fact. The NEL followed, and allowed itself to be absorbed into Chamberlain's National Liberal Federation of 1877, for which organization it had provided the model. (The real founder of the NLF, the Birmingham architect, William Harris, argued shrewdly that organizations such as the NEL or the Central Nonconformist Committee were now shown to be incapable of anything more than ephemeral political success). A little later Miall, now retired from the leadership of the Liberationists, urged the Society to stop working from 'an exclusively religious or Nonconformist point of view', and to think of itself as a ginger group within the Liberal Party. This, of course, came just after Dale and Rogers had intensified their Disestablishment campaign with a series of provincial tours, but Gladstone, who had realized the continuing potential of Dissent when it had blocked Forster's election as his successor in 1875, was now prepared, as in 1874, to draw the sting of Liberationism by appealing to the atavistic instincts of a wider Dissent.

There can be little doubt, as Guiness Rogers seemed to realize at the time, that one of the motives behind and results of the Bulgarian atrocities agitation was to woo the conscience-stricken Nonconformist vote away from confessional politics back to the generalized, highly moralistic Liberalism with which he everlastingly beguiled them. Dissent, already vexed with Disraeli over his Endowed Schools proposals and his rejection of their Burials Bill, was clearly prepared for a grand reconciliation. They recalled that long ago Palmerston had called the subject peoples of the Ottoman Empire 'the Nonconformists of Europe', and were reminded that the Christian Bulgars' difficulties with the Turkish authorities over the burial of their dead somehow resembled the Dissenters' own tribulations. Now, stirred up by W. T. Stead and Henry Richard, Dissenters of every description, from wealthy businessmen down to Joseph Arch's agricultural labourers unitedly took up the Bulgars as their 'special mission'. Gladstone was duly impressed with the moral fervour of this popular Nonconformity (probably never as 'popular' as he imagined it to be). He spoke emotionally of the 'new dimension of moral and political significance'

---

[23] S. M. Ingham, 'The Disestablishment Movement In England 1868–74' in *Journal of Religious History* iii (1964); H. J. Hanham, *Elections and Party Management* (1959), 117f; D. A. Hamer, *Liberal Politics In The Age of Gladstone and Roseberry* (1972), 6f.

which Dissent had now acquired: meetings between Gladstone and Nonconformist leaders now became regular occurrences, and moving tales were recounted of Anglican hardliners, such as E. A. Freeman, won over to the disestablishment cause by the force of Nonconformist moral fervour. Liberal unity was a reality once again. But for those with eyes to see, coming events were even now casting their shadows before. John Bright and Spurgeon were both unenthusiastic and took up ambivalent attitudes, while the stars of the campaign were undoubtedly Richard and his Welsh contingent, with English Nonconformity cast in a novel and subordinate role to this thwarted Celtic nationalism.[24]

For the 1880 General Election all the pressure groups with trifling exceptions united behind the Grand Old Man. Dale, Samuel Morley and Schnadhorst, as secretary of the CNC, were particularly prominent and Nonconformists forebore to make disestablishment an election issue, while clouding their Local Option dilemma with abstruse debates over compensation. Theirs was in consequence a resounding victory. Sixty-three Liberationists were elected and approximately half of the Liberal members had openly expressed sympathy for the removal of Nonconformist grievances. Gladstone, as in 1868, fulsomely congratulated the Dissenters on putting Liberal unity first and promised a programme of reform.[25]

The Burials Act of 1880 removed a very real and the very last of the Dissenters' hardships, most notably in the rural areas, where social and sectarian animosities were still pronounced. Once again, however, disillusionment with a Liberal government was bound to come sooner or later, and the Bradlaugh oath, foreign policy and licensing legislation very quickly opened up the cracks.

The prolonged Bradlaugh episode revealed that Nonconformity could never stay united for very long.[26] Samuel Morely's changing sides over Bradlaugh (pro in 1880, anti in 1882) was symptomatic of much deeper divisions and distresses. Congregational and radical Dissent were on the whole pro-Bradlaugh, the Methodists, who as late as 1880, the *Nonconformist* newspaper bemoaned, were still not proper Dissenters, generally anti-Bradlaugh and anti-Affirmation Bill. Spurgeon was anti- and neutral by turns. On the surface, however, there was this time no repetition of the widespread disaffection which characterized the First Ministry. 'Conscience' politics, with the Liberal Party seen as a kind of 'secular church' were by the early 80s the stock in trade of Nonconformist journalism, with Gladstone cast in the role of father figure to an admiring Dissent, and if he were too mild for the more left-wing Dissenters, then Chamberlain with his developing Unauthorized Programme of compulsory land purchase, fiscal reform and disestablishment (in effect the Birmingham civic gospel transposed

[24] R. T. Shannon, *Gladstone and The Bulgarian Agitation* (1963), *passim*.
[25] T. Lloyd, *The General Election of 1880* (1968), 114.
[26] W. L. Arnstein, *The Bradlaugh Case* (1965), 159–161.

onto a national platform) was an adequate substitute.[27] Once again, however, beneath the surface the splits were beginning to appear. Mundella as early as 1883 was lamenting the desertion of prominent Sheffield Wesleyans and Unitarians to the Tory ranks, while Shaw Lefevre, who was to lose his Reading seat in the 1885 election, attributed the poor showing of the Liberals in urban constituencies to the weakened role of Dissent in local radical politics. Certainly Liberal retreat in the towns may be thus partially explained.

In the countryside on the other hand the Party in 1885 carried all before it—a reflection perhaps of the change wrought by the legislation of 1884–85. The extension of the suffrage to the rural labourer had aroused hopes, particularly in Primitive Methodist breasts, of the final triumph of disestablishment and defeat of social injustice (the Primitives were generally two or three steps ahead of the more tepid Liberationist leadership), though whether or not the votes of radical Nonconformist rural labourers and mining villagers who were, Liberal Party-wise chronically ill-organized, counted for much as early as 1885 remains a moot point.[28] What is more certain is that to avert the threat of disestablishment and other horrors consequent upon this enlarged democracy, as well as to thwart Chamberlain's own ambition to be Liberal leader, Gladstone, shortly after the election was over, embraced Irish Home Rule. Did he, as Chamberlain believed, correctly foresee that this issue would permanently shatter Nonconformist political unity and so destroy their last chance of ever disestablishing the Church? If he reasoned thus, he was staging a gamble fraught with as many dangers for his entire Party as for its Nonconformist wing. In the traumas of 1885–86 Wesleyans and Unitarians were conspicuous in the Liberal- or Radical-Unionist ranks, the former not surprisingly as their conversion to Liberal politics had been belated and half-hearted, the latter for once forsaking the progressive side because of the presence of Chamberlain in their body.

Even the Baptists and Congregationals, who on the whole remained loyal to Gladstonianism, were not unaffected. Dale was among the first of the Unionists, a change of allegiance which was in 1888 to lead him to withdraw from the affairs of the Congregational Union. Newman Hall and Henry Allon sympathized with his stand. Among the Baptists Spurgeon's attitude was ambiguous, though he inclined to Unionism as did the more conservative elements in his denomination. Even the Quakers were divided, with John Bright, Lewis Fry, Arthur Pease and J. N. Richardson all turning Unionist, and F. L. Harris and

---

[27] From the standpoint of radical Dissent the Unauthorized Programme was certainly not new. Most of its provisions had been anticipated for many years in the various journals edited by the Baptist Benjamin Evans, particularly *The Church* (founded 1844) and *The Freeman* (1855). An evaluation of this mid-century radicalism is one of the major lacunae of Nonconformist historical writing.

[28] J. Howarth, 'The Liberal Revival In Northamptonshire' in *Historical Journal* xii (1969).

Alfred Bigland later taking their parliamentary seats on the Conservative benches. The annals of political turpitude could scarcely furnish
such awful instances—to those Dissenters for whom Gladstonianism
remained a way of life. The counsels of political Nonconformity seemed
permanently darkened.

Late Victorian

Of the seminal role of Nonconformity within Liberal and Radical
Unionism there can be little doubt. The Wesleyans need occasion no
surprise: anxious Liberals (and some historians after them) always
searched for the event which marked their 'final conversion' to political
Liberalism. It was, said some, the Bulgarian agitation of 1877, though
others fixed on Hughes's founding of the *Methodist Times* in 1885 as the
decisive point. In reality of course there was never any such mass
conversion. The Wesleyans' Tory/Imperialist streak remained ever
impervious to Liberal appeals.

But Nonconformist Unionists did not look to particular denominations but to a particular city. Though it was an obscure Liverpool
Wesleyan, William Oulton, who seems to have pioneered the movement in the provinces, it was in Chamberlain's own town that, as
M. C. Hurst has shown, the enormously complicated battle was fought
and won.[20] Here it was the skill of Dale (who, with his proposals for a
major Home Rule measure for Ireland with Irish members continuing
to sit at Westminster, nicely counterbalanced John Bright's hardline
approach which stood as far to the right of Chamberlain's own views
as Dale's to the left) which really won the Birmingham Liberal and
Radical Association for Unionism. Dale too was the power behind the
scenes in the abortive negotiations for Liberal reunion in 1887 (conducted significantly in the correspondence columns of *The Baptist*). With
John Albert Bright's victory in the Birmingham Central by-election of
1889 Chamberlain's personal triumph in his West Midlands 'Duchy'
was assured, and a power-base established from which the merger
with Conservatism, virtually complete by 1895, could be negotiated
from a position of strength. Obstacles there were a-plenty: denominational education, Welsh tithes, Local Option, and especially the
licensing clauses of the 1888 Local Government Act. But these things
Chamberlain's Nonconformist followers could apparently abide in
preference to Gladstone's fanatical dedication to the cause of Home
Rule.

In the country as a whole a Nonconformist Liberal Unionist
Association based on London made a certain amount of noise but
achieved little—there is only one recorded instance of a chapel being

[29] M. Hurst, 'Joseph Chamberlain and John Bright, 1886–89' in *Historical Journal*
vii (1964).

offered for one of its meetings. Nonconformists did not, however, wish to flaunt their Unionism in public, and the evidence of their defection from the Gladstonian camp must be sought in a myriad of local studies. Thus the Methodist farmers of Cornwall, as distinct from the miners, gravitated to Unionism quietly, sullenly, but with devasting effect at the polls, Chamberlain's Duchy certainly set the pattern for the East Midlands to follow in the later 90s, whilst F. B. Grotian, the Conservative member for East Hull, is found writing in 1887 of the overwhelmingly strong Nonconformist element in his constituency which he dared not alienate but which could apparently be forged into a valuable political asset.

One of the paradoxes of post-1885 politics is, however, that the shedding of these radical Unionists left the Nonconformists who continued loyal to Gladstone in a position of unwonted strength. The Whig aristocrats having departed, it was now left to local Nonconformist businessmen like J. J. Colman to play the role of local party magnate, social host and financial patron which the real-life equivalents of Trollope's Duke of Omnium had discharged in the past. The grip of the National Liberation Federation under its Quaker President, Robert Spence Watson, was also considerably tightened after the Home Rule split. Nonconformists were more prominent than ever before in the counsels, parliamentary and provincial, of the continuing Liberal Party. But whether the Nonconformist vote in the constituencies was comparably significant is very doubtful. In London, for example, those lower middle-class boroughs where Nonconformity was thought to be especially strong, Islington, Hackney, Lambeth and Peckham, registered no marked preference for the Liberals, and swam as strongly with the anti-Liberal tide in 1895 and 1900 as any other metropolitan constituencies. In Northamptonshire moreover, Dr Howarth finds that while the radical Nonconformists of Wellingborough and Kettering remained very active in the Liberal camp, their specifically Nonconformist politics had very little appeal in the villages which could not be roused over temperance, disestablishment or Home Rule and where sectarian politics simply could not be turned to Liberal advantage.[30]

The capitulation of English Liberalism to its Nonconformist wing is sometimes said to be highlighted by the Parnell crisis of 1889–90, when, we are told, Nonconformists deliberately used the Irish leader to drive Liberalism irreversibly into sectarian politics—after all the term 'the Nonconformist Conscience' was born during the Affair.[31] Yet if this was the result it was hardly the Nonconformists' intention at the outset.

[30] H. Pelling, *The Social Geography of British Elections, 1885–1910* (1967), 432f; M. Hurst, *Joseph Chamberlain and Liberal Reunion* (1967), *passim*; idem, *Joseph Chamberlain and West Midland Politics* (1962).
[31] J. F. Glaser, 'Parnell's Fall and The Nonconformist Conscience' in *Irish Historical Studies* xii (1960).

After a period of hesitation, Nonconformist leaders were constrained into taking a definite stand by a variety of overwhelming pressures: the silence of Parnell himself, the lead being taken out of their hands by E. T. Cook of the *Pall Mall Gazette*, Michael Davitt and others, the taunts of *The Times* and of the Tories, who saw in this a golden opportunity finally to detach Nonconformist Unionists from their Liberal brethren, the strange taciturnity of Gladstone, who possibly was anticipating with some relish a great Nonconformist-inspired moral crusade and an outburst of popular adulation such as had served him so well in 1876. Furthermore, disapproval of Parnell in 1890 was no Nonconformist fad: it was part of a complex national movement of moral revulsion embracing a wide spectrum of opinion from Cardinal Manning to Robert Blatchford.

Thus Nonconformists were placed in a cruel dilemma over Parnell which required no small exercise of political tact: instead, politically gauche as ever, they allowed Hugh Price Hughes to explode with bluster and bombast, and represent himself as the mouthpiece of the nation's moral conscience. Many Nonconformist leaders were indeed unhappy at the whole turn of events, J. G. Rogers, Henry Allon and the *British Weekly* in particular. (Alfred Illingworth became the one prominent Nonconformist to urge Parnell to stay on). But in the end it was the effervescent Hughes who carried the day, even to the extent of overruling his own private conviction that Parnell should in fact remain the Irish leader. Hughes now went on from strength to strength: the movement for Free Church unity which he now inspired had about it, as has been noted, his own peculiar hectoring and spiteful stamp, and was launched with the deliberate intention of finally crushing the establishment which he had sent reeling in 1890. But Hughes's more immediate triumph was the Liberals' adoption of the Newcastle programme in 1891, and the insertion of disestablishment and liquor clauses into the Party's manifesto.

Nonconformists considered the great Liberal electoral triumph of 1892 a vindication of their new-found aggression. For once they had proceeded with tact: there was, for example, no organized attempt to obstruct Dilke's candidature as there had been to bring down Parnell on similar grounds of outraged morality in 1890. As a result one hundred and nine Dissenters took their places on the Liberal benches in the new parliament (30 Methodists, 27 Congregationals, 11 Baptists, 10 Presbyterians, 10 Quakers, 20 Unitarians and one Swedenborgian). But the country had not really been converted to conscience politics. It was Gladstone's skilful manipulation of rural and urban discontent, particularly over the operation of the Poor Law, the growth of trade unionism and the proposals for local government reform which came to fruition in 1894–95 which had really won the day for the Liberals.

1892 was to prove for Nonconformity yet another false dawn. In the sorry tale of swift electoral alienation from the Liberals who had promised far more than they could perform, Nonconformity's role was conspicuous. The Conservatives especially exploited the 'faddism', as it was now dubbed, of this section of the Liberal Party to the embarrassment of the official leadership. Though in Parliament it was by now the Welsh Dissenters who made the running and Welsh rather than English disestablishment which aroused most Liberationist fervour, outside it was the gloomy and irrelevant sectarianism of the Nonconformist Liberals, set against a background of mounting economic distress which occasioned particular disquiet. Sometimes they behaved with chronic obtuseness, as in the campaign of the overbearing Mrs Ormiston Chant and the rather ridiculous Mr Shilton Collin, Liverpool tea merchant and Congregational, against the moral tone of the London theatres, especially the notorious Empire, in the mid-1890s. As J. F. Glaser remarks, 'Liberalism in the 1890s appeared to many working-class voters as a crotchet castle, from which dreary teetotaling Dissenters launched raids on pubs, music halls and politicians cited in divorce cases.'[32] The anticipated reward was reaped in the Tory victory of 1895 which, as Scott Holland declared, marked a most decisive public rejection of the politics of the Nonconformist conscience.

To this sorry tale the Free Churches' reaction to the Boer War makes a fitting climax. In the enflamed atmosphere of the times the type of Pro-Boerism sponsored by the *Daily News* not only attracted many Nonconformist ministers and their flocks but held out a variety of dangers—the dangers of physical assault to an extremist like Charles Aked, the outspoken Liverpool Baptist, the danger of dismissal to C. Sylvester Horne whose congregation took an opposing view to his own, the danger of charges of defeatism, treason and blackguardism for many others. But many Nonconformists, including some prominent ones, took the imperial side, as they had done in 1886. The Wesleyans, Hughes together with two influential laymen, Sir Henry Fowler (MP for Wolverhampton East) and R. W. Perks (MP for Louth) were naturally well to the fore, having stepped into the vacuum created by the ineptitude of other Nonconformist Liberals, and forged close links based on a shared imperialism with Lord Roseberry as early as 1894–95.[33] Having avowed his own sympathies so strongly, it was rather superfluous for Hughes to call stridently for official silence on an issue on which Freechurchmen were bitterly divided; the pro-Boers and particularly W. T. Stead could not remain inert in the face of what they felt to be a betrayal of Christian principles in an atmosphere of Jingoist extremism. The battle was fought out in the national press

[32] J. F. Glaser, 'English Nonconformity and The Decline of Liberalism' in *American Historical Review* lxiii (1957–58).

[33] S. Koss, 'Wesleyanism and Empire' in *Historical Journal* xviii (1) (1975). Koss underlines the aggressive imperialism of the Wesleyan politicians. In the General Election of 1900 seven Wesleyans were elected as Conservatives, eight as Liberal Imperialists, three as orthodox Liberals and three as old-fashioned Lib-Labs.

and in many a local conflict. (Where Dissenting Pro-Boerism was tinged with theological liberalism and imperialism with old-fashioned evangelicalism the battle of words was likely to be particularly exacerbated.) On this contentious and sour note and with, in 1900, another General Election defeat for the Liberals of grave proportions the Victorian era drew to its close.

There is one last consideration. Their significant role in the Liberal Party meant that Nonconformist attitudes to the rise of organized Labour would during the 1890s become of crucial importance to the future of radical politics in Great Britain. At the top Seebohm Rowntree and George Cadbury, as the Party's leading financiers and *éminences grises*, stood fairly to the left, accepting the movement for Old Age Pensions and other social reforms and advocating electoral cooperation with the nascent Labour movement, an attitude shared by these Quakers with Halley Stewart, the distinguished Congregational. Nor, considering the Nonconformist background of many of the early Socialists, Fred Jowett, Will Crooks, Arthur Henderson and Philip Snowdon, and the extent of Lib-Lab cooperation in cities, particularly in the London Progressive Party, was this mutual sympathy altogether surprising. A careful appraisal of Nonconformist press attitudes in the 1890s shows, however, that such an harmonization of interests was a rather artificial creation. It was the old Lib-Lab Trade Unionists like Henry Broadhurst of the stonemasons, men who shunned both the Eight Hour Day and the Minimum Wage, who elicited the most sympathy, while even the Primitive Methodists largely confined their sympathies to the unionism they believed themselves to have fathered, that of the farms and of the coal mines.

Nonconformity had thus hardly any role to play in the New Unionism of 1889 where in any case the unexpected intervention by Cardinal Manning had alarmed and confused them. Only Carlile of Bermondsey and Cuff of Shoreditch were openly sympathetic, while both H. P. Hughes and Clifford felt that Nonconformist help for the dockers had been too little and come too late. Perhaps, as H. W. Massingham wryly remarked in the *Daily News* in 1892, enthusiasm for the Bulgarian peasant came more easily to these people than sympathy for the London docker. By now, though in general sympathetic to Trade Unionism, always prepared to invite Union leaders to their assemblies and applaud their progressivist eloquence and to lend their powerful support to such causes as Old Age Pensions, the Dissenters, if their press is at all an accurate guide, were inclined to worry over the growing power of the TUC, its 'materialism' and the 'unreasonableness' of some of its demands, to condemn the strike weapon and, like the Primitive Methodist leadership in County Durham, to uphold the ideals of arbitration and conciliation, with copartnership as the long-term solution to industrial strife. Nonconformists rather complacently regarded Labour not as a separate political force but as a variant form of traditional radicalism, perhaps even an insurance that the Liberal Party would be compelled to remain radical. When the possibility of independent Labour initiative was mooted, Nonconformists reacted to such a suggestion with shock and incredulity. Patronage of the working-class movement remained their unquestioned assumption, the Settlement movement and the Institutional Church serving as models of what should be done within the Liberal movement as a whole.[34]

Dissenting rhetoric could not prevent an eventual parting of the ways between Liberal Nonconformists and Labour activists, and the years 1892–93 appear a decisive turning-point. For the Congregationals for example, the founding of the Union's Social Questions Committee in 1891 was followed the next year by the famous address by Keir Hardie to the Union Meeting at Bradford and by considerable social work during the miners' strike of 1893, but thereafter there is increasing wariness and suspicion on both sides, as the editorials in the *Nonconformist* and the *British Weekly* make clear. But the elderly Schnadhorst's unwillingness to see his organization transformed into a Lib-Lab Party and the unpopularity he occasioned through the paucity of Labour candidates in the 1892 election (which Labour leaders laid specifically at his door) had been inimical to smooth relationships. At the West Bradford contest of the same year, Ben Tillett openly fought the aged Alfred Illingworth, who a little later retired from the Liberal Party in protest against its growing collectivist trends. Alienation now proceeded rapidly till ten years later the Nonconformist press was so embarrassingly silent over the Taff Vale case that Socialists had perforce to enquire whether they were aware, not of its significance, but of its having happened at all?

It is now almost an accepted historical truism that the Passive Resistance campaign of 1902–05 was unexpected and adventitious, an 'artificial resurgence' of political Nonconformity, the last frenzied vapourings of moribund conscience politics. It is equally clear that despite their strength in the 1906 parliament the Liberal leadership now had the measure of the Nonconformists' potential, as the floundering of the Birrell, McKenna and Runciman Education Bills (1906, 07, 08) quickly showed.[35] Yet the pricking of the balloon may not have been so much a reaction to the impossible role they had cast for themselves within the Liberal ranks as a response to the decline of provincial Nonconformity as a factor of any political consequence whatsoever. Parker and Dale, as we have seen, desired that Nonconformists as individuals should play an active role in politics but abhorred the Free Churches *qua* churches entering the political arena, while Hughes,

[34] S. Mayor, *The Churches and The Labour Movement* (1967), 315f; G. W. Rusling, 'The Nonconformist Conscience' in *BQ* xxii (3) (1967).

[35] N. J. Richards, 'The Education Bill of 1906 and The Decline of Political Nonconformity' in *J Ecc H* xxiii (1972); E. A. Payne, 'The Religious Education Dilemma' in *BQ* xxiii (8) (1970).

never backward in political utterance himself, felt that for the health of the churches a discreet political silence ought to be preserved by the denominational spokesman on contentious issues. It is a measure of how far Nonconformity had travelled that by 1909, when an influential but anonymous tract *Nonconformity and Politics* issued from the press, the author could regard it as most wholesome and natural that Dissenters should have no politics at all. The wheel had come full circle: in 1809 too, such sentiments would have been commonplace—in most of the intervening years they would have been greeted outside the conventicles of pietists and minority sects with hostility and derision.

Conclusion

Strangerhood's deliverance: Nonconformist philanthropy and mutual aid

If affairs of state reveal Victorian Dissent at its most self-deceivingly ineffectual, it is safe to assume on the evidence of recent research that their record in local politics is far happier, and their achievement in philanthropy, particularly in an urban context, more impressive still. Many a contemporary who like the Liverpool Presbyterian, 'Ian Maclaren', found a surrogate for private intellectual doubts in an energetic round of charitable activities could publicly excuse his theological difficulties by declaring that 'though the world often finds one's profession of faith hard to comprehend, it can always understand service.'

Unfortunately in the present historiographical climate no aspect of Victorianism lies under a more disapproving cloud than its zeal for well-doing. Victorian philanthropy, we are told, took it for granted that poverty sprang from moral failure, looked at effects not causes, and so made a superficial and unimaginative diagnosis of social ills, was top-heavy with administrators, reputation-seekers and persons who regarded charitable fund-raising activities as steps to social prestige, even as part of the social round. Full of righteous indignation and comforting words, it spurned analysis, comparative investigations, and case studies. It had in addition a strange set of priorities: sailors, criminals and children in descending order. By highlighting the generosity of the rich and the inadequacies of the poor, it created a servile and cringing class of recipients, and as W. J. Fox, the lapsed Unitarian, and one of philanthropy's earliest critics, was among the first to point out, it directed attention away from radical social change and thus helped to preserve an unjust social order. So reads the indictment—but how far does Nonconformity conform to this horrific model?

This question can not be answered till it is realized that the Dissenters, wittingly or not, created their own model of what should constitute the philanthropic outworking of their religious convictions. They held, firstly, that social work and evangelism were the obverse and reverse of the same spiritual coin: soul-winning meant changed men, and changed men a changed environment. And if, as the century wore on, a changed environment was seen by increasing numbers as a prerequisite for, rather than a tribute to, successful evangelism, the two remained inextricably linked.

Secondly, their idea of philanthropy centred round the associative principle rather than, on the one hand, individual ameliorative work (though the more individualistic Dissenters, particularly the Baptists, were happiest with the latter) or, on the other, collective prevention (though the more radical and liberal Quakers and Unitarians were being driven to this in the last two decades of the century).

Thirdly, philanthropy, like municipal politics, was not considered by Nonconformists an optional leisure time activity in which they could indulge to assuage guilty feelings, impress their neighbours or swim with the powerful secular currents of their age: rather philanthropy should broadcast the essential quality of their religious societies, should reflect the mutual aid, the bearing and sharing of one another's burdens, which characterized the self-help of the chapel community at its very best.

Fourthly, continually aware of the Catholics' appeal to salvation by merit and of their regarding their own good works as superior in every sense to Protestantism's, Nonconformists were intent on proving that in fact the reverse was true, and that it was in the carefully premeditated quality of *their* philanthropy that they could best exhibit their moral superiority to Popery.

Fifthly, the charitable impulse, as might be expected, varies considerably in character between the different denominations. The Quakers were both first in the field and predominant throughout the early part of the century. At first under tutelage to the Anglican Evangelicals from whom they learnt their techniques of rousing public opinion and pressurizing government, the Friends, particularly Elizabeth Fry, William Allen, Joseph Cropper and Joseph Sturge, were at the centre of the whole network of early nineteenth-century organizations, Abolitionist and Penal Reform agitations, the Peace Society, and bodies for assisting Distressed Manufacturers and for the Relief and Benefit of the Manufacturing and Labouring Poor.

The Quakers, however, had not the numerical strength to sustain these endeavours, which were in any case largely the fruits of the new evangelical Quakerism of the Gurneys and related families. Peace activity withered after the Crimean War, the Anti-Slavery movement broke up in recriminations over the Sugar Tariffs and the use of force in slavery suppression. But the zeal for penal reform was continued in the Howard Association (founded 1866) of which the Quaker William Tallack was first secretary, Friends such as Robert Backhouse and Edward Charleton lent their full weight to Josephine Butler's Moral Purity crusade, the extension of Adult Education became their 'special calling', while later still the Rowntrees, Peases, Grubbs and the influential convert Stephen Hobhouse were experimenting with very radical ideas (in contrast to the older types of Quaker philanthropists like John Horniman or the ex-Quakers turned Anglicans, the Hanburys, Gurneys and Barclays). In many ways Quakers were far ahead of their time: Allen's investigation into the living conditions of Spitalfields in 1812 was a pioneering exercise in scientific case work, not lost on other Friends. In other ways, however, the Quakers tend to conform, sometimes grotesquely so, to the hostile model outlined above: both Francis Place and Cobden commented savagely on their love of the social distinction which their philanthropic activities brought them: the Peases, Brights and Ashworths have moreover a particularly sorry record as opponents of Factory Legislation.

The Unitarians became prominent in philanthropic work firstly through their medical and educational charities of the Napoleonic War period, secondly through their sponsoring of Mechanics' Institutes and thirdly through their Domestic Mission movement of the 1830s and 40s. It was this last which really focussed public attention on their charitable ideals. Combining the insights of the Scots Presbyterian Dr Thomas Chalmers and the American Transcendentalist Joseph Tuckerman, the Missions, set in the poorest parts of the great cities, had as their objectives not merely the cultivation of self-help or mutual aid among the needy (this they shared with the Evangelicals) but an unusually strident insistence that the Mission should be the point at which class barriers should be breached, rich and poor learn from one another and civic community be truly realized. Unitarians began now in grim earnestness to espouse a variety of good works: special schools, public baths and washhouses, parks and recreational rooms, provident clubs, district nursing, the reclamation of the evil-liver. All the time they growled at the opulence and philistinism of fellow business-men and industrialists as rich as they, yet falsely secure in their sub-urban fastnesses and indifferent to the slums: 'howl, ye rich' became William Rathbone VI of Liverpool's favourite word of rebuke for his fellow magnates.

Inevitably, as intelligent and widely read philanthropists having widespread interests in so many fields, commercial, educational and cultural, the Unitarians were the first to realize the inadequacies of overlapping charities and the frauds to which this led, and to press for rationalization and centralization of philanthropic endeavour. The Charity Organization Society of 1869 was very much their brainchild, even if they did not wholly share its subsequent evoking of the principles of 1834. But the COS, whatever its policies, was enough of a bureau-cratic machine to stifle the warmth and intimacy of that personal contact between rich and poor at which the Domestic Mission Move-ment had always aimed. When the same William Rathbone began to apologize that in his enthusiasm for planning he must seem 'like a socialist', and his young friend Charles Booth discovered that somehow Unitarian charitable effort had the activism of Martha but somehow lacked the spirit of Mary, they were confessing that their religious isolation as Unitarians was reinforced by a growing alienation from the very classes with which they had tried hardest to identify. And herein lay their tragedy.

The third of the major denominations to set the pace in charitable provision was the Wesleyans, but because they were such a self-contained 'Holy Community', a state within a state almost, and hugged their institutions close to their own bosoms, their record in this field has gone largely unrecorded. But from the 1790s when they expressed their founder's 'catholic christianity' in bodies such as the Strangers Friend Society, in work among the lowest and most depraved, in the Night Asyla of the great towns, amongst navvies and wandering Irish, up to the time of a later flowering of these same impulses in the central missions of the 80s and 90s, the Wesleyans, despite both their painful divisions and their growing wealth, never lost sight of their original mission to the most downcast and degraded elements of all. And to those other Methodists who shared their original insights they were an unfailing inspiration.

As for the Wesleyans, so for other orthodox Dissenters—the charitable impulse swelled when revivalism was in the ascendant, and died down in times of spiritual torpor. This is a sixth feature of Nonconformist philanthropy which is now becoming apparent to all historians except those perverse ones who presuppose that religious revival must always be detrimental to social progress. It is no accident, for example, that when Congregational Home Missionary enthusiasm was at its height about 1807, the London Female Penitentiary at Pentonville was pioneered by members of this body, or that first Charles Finney and then Moody confidently linked an upsurge of philanthropic work with their evangelistic success. The Keswick Conventions were as much meetings of philanthropists as of earnest spiritual seekers. None of the great names in late nineteenth century Nonconformity, Congregational, Baptist or Presbyterian, Morley, Herschell, Samuel Smith, Pilkington, Pye-Smith, Spicer, Wills, Curwen or Colman, escaped the inspiration of the Moody-Sankey revival—several in fact first discovered their passion for personal evangelism and social service through this very agency.

There is however a seventh aspect to the Nonconformist philanthropy of the Victorian period, and one in which its leaders legitimately took most pride: the extension of the bounds of citizenship to classes hitherto outside the social pale: drunkards and lunatics, orphans and prostitutes, tramps and sweeps. All these groups evangelical and particularly Nonconformist charity brought within the sphere of public concern for the first time, a social revolution scarcely less significant than the gradual extension of the franchise during the same period.

They wrought their work through a plethora of different missions and institutions. The downtown Missions were the prime agencies in the work. To the clusters of local organizations, maternity societies, sewing classes, ragged schools, evening classes, soup kitchens, free breakfasts and the like, Nonconformist churches began to add from the 1860s onwards other, more sophisticated bodies. In London, for example, Richard Weaver and Reginald Ratcliffe, two free-lance evangelists, founded the East End Mission and Relief Committee (1860), emigration societies appeared with a salutary emphasis on the family unit and a careful provision of employment opportunities in the receiving colonies, the Quakers pioneered the Bradford Institute (for adult education work especially) in 1865, the Baptists missions in connexion with Bloomsbury and Regent's Park Chapels and the Metropolitan Tabernacle from which the famous Stockwell Orphange also arose, the Methodists took over disused dance halls or public houses and founded the Leysian Mission and the Bermondsey Settlement, while the Presbyterians made their Regent's Square Chapel the centre of an impressive complex of relief agencies.

The appearance of the *Bitter Cry of Outcast London* in 1883 was an additional spur to these endeavours. Once again the denominational responses were all rather different. The Methodists' combination of tightly-knit and closely supervised evangelism and rescue work was probably unique, the Baptists rather conservatively concentrated all their work on a particular congregation rather than adopt a community approach (though F. B. Meyer at Christ Church was exceptional here), the Congregationals, on the other hand, allowed their Browning and Mansfield Settlements to become too separate, too amorphous and too heavily involved in politics for their spiritual good. Needless to say the metropolitan experiments were reflected in the provinces: the work of J. B. Paton in Nottingham, Samuel Smith in Liverpool and F. W. Crossley in Manchester are reminders of that.

Greater sophistication marked the work of the Missions as time went on, and this is seen particularly in the increasing use of trained social workers and the refinement of medical mission work, whose growth is a marked feature of the last three decades of the century. Though the inspiration of the Anglican Evangelicals is paramount in this field, that of Elizabeth Fry's Institute of Nursing (1841), Agnes Jones' and William Rathbone's introduction of domiciliary nursing into Liverpool in the 1860s, and the Reverend Andrew Reed's (Congregational) provision of Home For Incurables (a notable step forward in the history of geriatric medicine) counted for much in the development of medical mission work and dispensaries in the later Victorian town. The medical missions were overlapping, eccentrically selective and spasmodic, and so gave particular offence to the tidy minds of the Webbs: those who used their services doubtless felt otherwise.

The Nonconformists' had had a particular concern for the young, ever since the Unitarian John Pounds of Portsmouth had anticipated Shaftesbury's Ragged Schools earlier in the century. (The Ragged Schools in provincial towns were in any case more usually run by

Nonconformists than by Evangelical Anglicans.) It was Wesleyan experience in pioneering infant education which led to the development in the towns of crèches and nurseries which anticipate the work of Rachel Macmillan, while Nonconformists of many types sponsored recreational institutions, uniformed organizations and Shoeblack Brigades as a cure for teenage unemployment and delinquency. The YMCA was a wholly evangelical creation: the Police Court Missions of the 1870s and later, a sphere in which Congregationals and Baptists were especially prominent, not only led on directly to the modern Probation Service but challenged contemporary harshness with their novel emphasis on aftercare and rehabilitation. The same motive lies behind the provision of Reformatories and Industrial Schools for young offenders as an alternative to prison, though here evangelical Dissenters were rather suspicious of the prominence of Mary Carpenter and her Unitarian friends. Orphanages were a special concern of the more conservative types of evangelical Dissenters. Spurgeon's at Stockwell was only one of many: Dr Barnardo, Mr Fegan and George Muller of Bristol were all Brethren, while Dr Stephenson from a background of Wesleyan pietism not only founded the National Children's Homes but helped transform the somewhat bleak and forbidding orphange idea into the happier, more child-centred approach of the cottage–or scattered-homes of the last two decades of the century.

For the outcasts of society, for prisoners and prostitutes, the Nonconformists evinced a similar concern. The work of the Quaker penal reformers would have been fruitless but for the after-care services provided later on in the century by the various Prison Gates Missions. Josephine Butler's crusades of the 70s and 80s were backed up most vigorously by Unitarians, especially the Stansfelds, and by Bramwell Booth, though odium theologicum entered here also when Evangelicals founded their Gospel Purity Association (1884) to rival the mainly Unitarian Social Purity Alliance (1874). Even so it was the Midnight Movement and the provision of Rescue Homes, pioneered in the 1860s by Nonconformists such as Baptist Noel, Dr Brock, Newman Hall and Catherine Booth, which made the later Purity Crusade possible.

The handicapped were another class for whom Dissenters realized that the contemporary Poor Law made no provision. Schools, homes and workshops for the blind, provision for the deaf and the crippled, and the improved treatment of lunatics were all good works pioneered by the Clapham sect. But here rival religious and political movements interacted with beneficial results. Legislation on behalf of the afflicted was usually prepared by Utilitarians: its interpretation and application often fell to Shaftesbury himself, while in the provinces it was generally the Nonconformist agencies which had both to search out the handicapped, and make provision for their needs. Here the work of two Congregational ministers, the Reverend Thomas Arnold of Nottingham who laboured on behalf of the deaf and of Andrew Reed in the interests of mentally defective children, is a forerunner to the efforts of the Unitarian Mary Dendy later on in the century.

Finally, mention should be made of the Nonconformists' concern for particular social and occupational groups. For sailors it was the Wesleyans who had always shown especial concern, but it was a Baptist, the Reverend G. C. Smith, who built up the Bethel Seamen's Union with its 'floating chapels' and shore establishments in the 1820s. It was the Wesleyans again who, particularly after the Crimean War, provided recreational institutions for soldiers in garrison towns, while organizations such as the Christian Excavators' Union (1877), the Railway Mission (1881), the Cabmen's Club Aid Society (1859) and the Christian Police Association (1883) arose out of the specialized missions to different groups which have been noted as a feature of later Victorian revivalism.

It is in connection with these myriad evangelistic activities that an eighth feature of Nonconformist philanthropy which is possibly the undergirding of the whole endeavour, becomes apparent. Whatever the sickliness and maudlin quality of their ideal of domesticity, Victorian Dissenters rendered no greater service to their contemporaries than by the transplantation of the 'home' principle into the rigorous world of the early Victorian charitable institutions. It was they who, as Dr Heasman insists, in fulfilment of their best and most basic insights, transformed the juvenile asylum into the children's home, the penitentiary into the rescue home, the almshouse into the Old People's home, and who through their tracts and magazines prepared public and parliamentary opinion for progressive legislative change. Whatever their other inadequacies, for this achievement at least they deserve belated recognition.

Select Bibliography

(The place of publication is London, except where otherwise stated).

General; There are a number of older surveys of nineteenth-century Dissent which are still useful, if only because the authors were deeply involved in the issues and controversies of the times. Such are H. S. Skeats and C. S. Miall, *History of the Free Churches of England, 1688–1891* (n.d.), C. S. Horne, *Popular History of the Free Churches* (1903) and *Nonconformity in the XIXth Century* (1905), and W. B. Selbie, *Nonconformity, Its Origin and Progress* (1912). H. W. Clark, *History of English Nonconformity Vol. 2* (1913) introduces a sadder, more critical note. More recent introductions to the subject include two reflective essays written during the War years: H. L. Cocks, *The Nonconformist Conscience* (1943) and E. A. Payne, *The Free Church Tradition in the Life of England* (1944). H. Davies, *The English Free Churches* (1953) is also useful. Three other books were written in celebration of the Tercentenary of the Great Ejection: E. Routley, *English Religious Dissent* (Cambridge 1960), F. G. Healey, *Rooted in Faith* (1961) and J. T. Wilkinson, *1662 And After* (1962). For the non-aligned who find the Nonconformist tradition difficult to understand, C. Driver, *A Future For the Free Churches?* (1962) and K. Young, *Chapel* (1972) are invaluable, though on specific details the latter should be used with caution.

Documentary Collections. D. Nicholls, *Church and State in Britain since 1820* (1967) is useful for the Disestablishment and related campaigns, while more generally D. M. Thompson, *Nonconformity In The Nineteenth Century* (1972) approaches the subject from a chronological angle, and J. H. Y. Briggs and I. Sellers, *Victorian Nonconformity* (1973) provide a wide-ranging impressionistic survey.

Individual Denominations; Wesleyanism has received a disproportionate amount of attention from the historians. B. Gregory's rather scurrilous *Sidelights on the Conflicts of Methodism, 1827–52* (1898) should be read alongside the more sober official account in W. J. Townsend, H. B. Workman and G. Eayrs, *A New History of Methodism*, 2 Vols (1909). M. Edwards, *After Wesley* (1935) and *Methodism and England* (1943), E. R. Taylor, *Methodism and Politics, 1791–1851* (Cambridge 1935) and W. J. Warner, *The Wesleyan Movement in the Industrial Revolution* (1930) attempt to understand Wesleyanism in a wider social context. J. Kent, *The Age of Disunity* (1966) is as deeply sympathetic as W. R. Ward, *Religion and Society in England, 1790–1850* (1972) is penetrating, while B. Semmel, *The Methodist Revolution* (1974) sees English Wesleyanism against a background of worldwide ideological upheaval. J. C. Bowmer, *Pastor and People* (1975) presents an unfashionable 'high' view of Wesleyan history. In comparison with all this the historian of radical Methodism must still rely on H. B. Kendall, *Origin and History of the Primitive Methodist Church*, 2 Vols (n.d.) and *A History of the Primitive Methodist Church* (1919), on G. Packer, *Centenary of the Methodist New Connexion* (1897), O. A. Beckerlegge, *The United Methodist Free Churches* (1957) and T. Shaw, *The Bible Christians* (1965) for these respective traditions. Fortunately R. F. Wearmouth's enthusiastic if uncritical *Methodism and the Working Class Movements of England, 1800–1850* (1937) and *Methodism and the Struggle of the Working Classes, 1850–1900* (Leicester 1954) and R. Currie's brilliant but caustic *Methodism Divided* (1968) gives full weight to the Methodist sects.

Congregationalism is surveyed through Union office windows by A. Peel, *These Hundred Years* (1931) and more recently by a sympathetic Welsh Independent, R. T. Jones in his *Congregationalism in England, 1662–1962* (1962). The Baptists are covered by A. C. Underwood, *A History of the English Baptists* (1947) and E. A. Payne, *The Baptist Union. A Short History* (1959), the latter work being of much wider interest than its title would imply. A new denominational history is in preparation. Unitarian historians have written extensively on their particular tradition. R. V. Holt's catalogue-like *Unitarian Contribution to Social Progress* (1938) should be read alongside the more analytical treatment provided by E. M. Wilbur, *A History of Unitarianism, Vol 2* (Cambridge, Mass. 1952), C. G. Bolam and others, *The English Presbyterians* (1968) and D. G. Wigmore-Beddoes, *Yesterday's Radicals* (Cambridge 1971). For the orthodox Presbyterians the standard work remains the now outdated A. H. Drysdale, *History of Presbyterianism in England* (1889), though for the Society of Friends E. Isichei, *Victorian Quakers* (Oxford 1970) is a model of how Nonconformist history should be written. The Brethren are well treated by H. H. Rowdon, *The Origins of the Brethren* (1967) and F. R. Coad, *A History of the Brethren Movement* (1968). For the smaller bodies R. Sandall and A. R. Wiggins, *History of the Salvation Army, 1865–1914, 5 Vols* (1947–68), J. Vickers, *History of Independent Methodism* (Newton-le-Willows 1920) and A. C. Watters, *History of the British Churches of Christ* (Indianapolis, 1947) are all useful.

Theology, Liturgy, Architecture; Horton Davies, *Worship And Theology in England, Vol 3, Fom Watts and Wesley to Maurice* (Princeton and London 1961), and *Vol 4, From Newman to Martineau* (Princeton and London 1962) remain the best introduction to these related subjects, though these works may be supplemented for the historical theology of nineteenth century Dissent by W. B. Glover, *Evangelical Nonconformists and Higher Criticism in the Nineteenth Century* (1954) and J. W. Grant, *Free Churchmanship in England, 1870–1940* (n.d), for its liturgical developments by A. E. Peaston, *The Prayer Book Tradition in the Free Churches* (1964) and for its architecture by R. P. Jones, *Nonconformist Church Architecture* (1914), M. S. Briggs, *Puritan Architecture and its Future* (1946) and K. Lindley, *Chapels and Meeting Houses* (1969).

Politics and Sociology; Of general interest here are B. L. Manning, *The Protestant Dissenting Deputies* (Cambridge 1952) and from a much broader perspective K. S. Inglis, *Churches and the Working Classes in Victorian England* (1963). For the earlier period R. Cowherd, *The Politics of English Dissent* (1959), U. R. Q. Henriques, *Religious Toleration in England, 1787–1833* (1961) and R. W. Davies, *Dissent in Politics, The Political Life of William Smith M.P.* (1971) are all-important, while S. Mayor, *The Churches and the Labour Movement* (1967) and W. H. Mackintosh, *Disestablishment and Liberation* (1972) throw much light on the later Victorian years. J. D. Gay, *The Geography of Religion in England* (1971) and A. Everitt, *The Pattern of Rural Dissent; The Nineteenth Century* (Leicester 1972) are welcome pioneering works on ecclesiastical geography. For individual towns E. R. Wickham, *Church and People in an Industrial City* (*Sheffield*) (1957) and A. Brockett, *Nonconformity in Exeter* (Manchester 1962) are sympathetic and balanced, and E. P. Hennock, *Fit and Proper Persons* (1973) has much light to throw on the complexities of Birmingham Dissent. Other urban or regional surveys are to be found in articles and unpublished University theses.

Index